<sup>auew</sup> **tass**

# Computer Technology and Employment

PUBLISHED BY NCC PUBLICATIONS

**NCC**
The National Computing Centre

The National Computing Centre develops techniques and provides aids for the more effective use of computers. NCC is a non-profit distributing organisation backed by government and industry. The Centre

—co-operates with, and co-ordinates the work of, members and other organisations concerned with computers and their use

—provides information, advice and training

—supplies software packages

—promotes standards and codes of practice

Any interested company, organisation or individual can benefit from the work of the Centre by subscribing as a member. Throughout the country, facilities are provided for members to participate in working parties, study groups and discussions, and to influence NCC policy. A regular journal — 'NCC Interface' — keeps members informed of new developments and NCC activities. Special facilities are offered for courses, training material, publications and software packages.

For further details get in touch with the Centre at Oxford Road, Manchester M1 7ED (telephone 061-228 6333)

or at one of the following regional offices:

| Belfast | 1st Floor | Glasgow | 2nd Floor |
|---|---|---|---|
| | 117 Lisburn Road | | Anderston House |
| | BT9 7BP | | Argyle Street |
| Telephone: | 0232 665997 | | G2 8LR |
| | | Telephone: | 041-204 1101 |

| Birmingham | 2nd Floor | London | 11 New Fetter Lane |
|---|---|---|---|
| | Prudential Buildings | | EC4A 1PU |
| | Colmore Row | Telephone: | 01-353 4875 |
| | B3 2PL | | |
| Telephone: | 021-236 6283 | | |

| Bristol | 6th Floor |
|---|---|
| | Royal Exchange Building |
| | 41 Corn Street |
| | BS1 1HG |
| Telephone: | 0272 27077 |

# Foreword

The computer industry is of growing significance to the UK and world economy. As a result of its development we are on the threshold of a technological revolution as important as the invention of the wheel, power-looms, electricity and the assembly line.

There are however major differences from the circumstances of the first industrial revolution. On the one hand the new technology is controlled by transnational companies, whose attempts to bring about a new international division of labour are not necessarily in the UK's interests. On the other hand Labour movements called into being in response to the social costs demanded by the earlier industrialisation are no longer prepared to pay this price. They are therefore taking an increasingly active role in controlling the further development of the technology.

In order to contribute to union thinking on the impact of computer technology and microelectronics on employment, AUEW(TASS) convened an Advisory Conference on the 16th September, 1978. Present were active members of the union with senior positions in computer production or application throughout the UK Engineering industry. An abridged version of the Conference Proceedings, and the background papers circulated are contained in this book. It is published as a contribution to the public debate on this matter, which needs to culminate in action to ensure that the new technology leads to more employment, more purchasing power and more leisure for working people and their families.

KEN GILL
*General Secretary*
AUEW(TASS)

Keywords for information retrieval (drawn from the
*NCC Thesaurus of Computing Terms*): Trade Unions, Impact (computer),
Microelectronics, Microprocessors

| British Library Cataloguing in Publication Data |
| --- |
| Computer Technology and Employment. *Conference*, London, 1978 Computer technology and employment. 1. Labor supply – Great Britain – Congresses 2. Automation – Economic aspects – Great Britain – Congresses 3. Microprocessors – Economic aspects – Great Britain – Congresses I. Amalgamated Union of Engineering Workers. Technical, Administrative and Supervisory Section 331.1    HD5765.A6 ISBN 0-85012-212-0 |

**Disclaimer**

First published in 1979 by:
NCC Publications, The National Computing Centre Limited,
Oxford Road, Manchester M1 7ED, England, and
AUEW(TASS), Onslow Hall, Little Green, Richmond, Surrey.

ISBN 0-85012-212-0

This book is set in 10/11 pt. Times Roman Series
and printed by John Goodman & Sons (Printers) Ltd.,
64 Cardigan Street, Birmingham B4 7RS, England.

# Participants

**Speakers**

| | |
|---|---|
| Benson, Ian | National Computer Industry Advisory Panel |
| Bloomfield, C | Rumbelows (Thorn) |
| Booth, Albert, Rt Hon | Secretary of State for Employment |
| Burgess, J | British Aerospace (Hatfield) |
| Cheyvialle, M | CII Honeywell-Bull (France), CGT |
| Clyne, L | Logica |
| Cooke, J | Ford Motor Company |
| Cooper, R | GEC |
| Cowey, A | British Shipbuilders |
| Gage, P | Baker Perkins |
| Hardie, R | Ferranti |
| Holton, J | Davy International |
| Lancashire, Eric | Rolls Royce (Derby) |
| Lapeyre, M | CFDT (France), National Secretary |
| Lindsay, R | Chubb Gross Cash |
| Lombardi, M | Olivetti (Italy), FLM |
| Luck, P M | Smiths Industries |
| Marshall, A | Plessey Telecommunications |
| McMillan, Denise | GEC |
| Meaney, Vera | Rumbelows (Thorn) |
| Mehrens, K | DGB (IG Metall), Germany |
| Painter, J R | British Aerospace (Hatfield) |
| Parr, I | ICI |
| Rowan, John | AUEW(TASS) National Industrial Officer |
| Shutt, J D | Chrysler |
| Starrs, Des | AUEW(TASS) President |
| Tuchfeld, John | AUEW(TASS) National Industrial Officer |
| Turner, J | ICL |
| Warburton, T | GEC |
| Ward, P | AUEW(TASS) Vice President |
| Wootton, C | National Women's Committee |
| York, J | NCR |

## Other Participants

| | |
|---|---|
| Arrowsmith, D | Northern Engineering Industries |
| Bridger, J | National Technical Committee |
| Bullen, R M | ITT |
| Di-Siena, G | Cambridge Instruments |
| Foster, J | Automotive Products |
| Grainger, H | Weir Group |
| Hogg, J | Vickers |
| Hood, W | Tube Investments |
| Imrie, J | Burroughs |
| James, K A | BICC |
| John, H | British Steel Corporation |
| Johnson, D V | EMI |
| Kanner, D | Coltec Data Systems |
| Leeson, W G | Dunlop |
| Linton, J | Burroughs |
| McKenchie, R | Ferranti |
| Myles, M | ICL |
| Niven, W | AUEW(TASS) National Industrial Officer, National Management Committee |
| Parkes, J | Lucas |
| Robinson, E | Vauxhall |
| Sadler, B C | Petbow |
| Seager, B | National Computer Industry Advisory Panel |
| Skidmore, P | GKN |
| Smith, C D | GEC |
| Smith, J | Honeywell |
| Steele, L | GEC |
| Thomas, R | British Leyland |
| Van Der Schraft, H | Avery |

# Contents

*Page*

**Foreword**

**Participants**

**PART 1 – CONFERENCE PROCEEDINGS**

**1 Opening Remarks**      13

**2 Technology and Society**      15

**3 Discussion**      25

**4 The View from Western Europe**      37
German Metalworkers      37
Italian Metalworkers      39
French Metalworkers      40

**5 Technology and Union Policy**      47
Health and Safety      47
Cash Registers      48
Telecommunications      49
Petrochemicals      52
Word Processing      53
Social Implications      54
Sex Discrimination      56
Aerospace      58
Computer-Aided Design      59
National Enterprise Board      62
Shipbuilding      63
Alternative Technology      63
Computer Staff Organisation      65

**6 Closing Remarks**      67

*Page*

**PART 2 – BACKGROUND PAPERS**

  7 **Questionnaire**            75

  8 **The Impact of Computer Technology**          79

  9 **The Changeover to Electronics**       101

10 **The Structure of the Electronics Industry**       117

11 **Computer-Aided Administration**       127

12 **Computer-Aided Design**       133

13 **Computer-Aided Manufacture in Batch Production**       151

**APPENDIX**

  **Glossary of Computer Terms**       161

# Part 1
# Conference Proceedings

1 **Opening Remarks**
2 **Technology and Society**
3 **Discussion**
4 **The View from Western Europe**
   German Metalworkers
   Italian Metalworkers
   French Metalworkers
5 **Technology and Union Policy**
   Health and Safety
   Cash Registers
   Telecommunications
   Petrochemicals
   Word Processing
   Social Implications
   Sex Discrimination
   Aerospace
   Computer-Aided Design
   National Enterprise Board
   Shipbuilding
   Alternative Technology
   Computer Staff Organisation
6 **Closing Remarks**

# 1   Opening remarks

## Des Starrs

The Executive Committee of TASS decided early in 1978 to revise the 1976 policy statement of computers

— to bring it up-to-date with changing technology and industrial structure, and

— to incorporate guidelines to the membership in controlling the use of computer-based machinery.

Partly as a result of TASS work in the NEDC, the sector working parties and the TUC, there has been a great widening of concern about technical change. The 1978 TUC Congress debated the subject and unanimously carried a resolution, seconded by TASS and in line with its policy in calling for particular attitudes to be struck by the TUC.

The resolution urges the General Council to press the Government to:

1 establish and develop a viable and soundly researched British research development and substantial manufacturing capacity in the field of microprocessors and allied computer systems

2 provide sufficient specialised training facilities to meet the manpower and manufacturing requirements of its hardware and software applications

3 develop forward plans at both national and local levels to ensure the maintenance and if possible the expansion of job opportunities in those areas adversely affected

4 carry out as a high priority a comprehensive study of the employment and social consequences of advances in the new microelectric technology and similar advances in the UK technology together with the wider ramifications of its application by our competitors

5 give consideration to the opportunities which may be offered as a result of the new technology for greater leisure time

6 establish pre-emptive schemes of training, labour-intensive and life-long educational job creation, so as to allow the transfer to high technology society to proceed smoothly

7 declare publicly their concern at the prospects of the resulting unemployment and support the move towards a shorter working week, month, year or life-time, with no deterioration in living standards

8 co-operate with overseas trade unions and governments, both developed and less developed, so as to get an international agreement to an international problem.

Congress went on to call on the General Council to prepare a draft policy statement in consultation with affiliated unions for a conference on this subject and to report to the 1979 Congress.

The present TASS conference is considering how far computerisation has already developed, what its effects have been, and at what rate the process is accelerating. Attention is given to which industrial sectors are threatened as well as to which sectors might grow. In this way we hope to gain some insight into the likely impact on employment, and stimulate the wider debate within the union, and the labour movement, to ensure that the process of technical change is beneficial to working people and their families.

# 2 Technology and society

**Rt Hon Albert Booth**

It is most significant that in organising the conference it has been seen as totally appropriate to invite fraternal delegates from a number of unions from other countries. This is, as the TUC have declared in their resolution, an international problem, and it is important to seek an international solution. Unions and governments in countries with advanced economies have a major responsibility to play national roles which supplement any international solutions.

On grounds of efficiency, equity and humanity, the achievement and maintenance of full employment should be the policy aim of every British government, of whatever complexion. It is probably a more heart-felt aspiration in the Labour movement than for its opponents, not least because the scourge of unemployment has been such a significant factor in the development of the movement. Political argument focusses on the role of the state: should there be massive state intervention to combat unemployment, or should the state withdraw, as Keith Joseph would argue, to let privately-owned enterprise develop at will?

We are being increasingly forced to recognise that the level of employment in our economy is not within the exclusive control of the British government. We certainly have less control than we would like. Countries are increasingly interdependent: in the economic sphere we are ever more vulnerable to decisions, trends and developments that originate elsewhere in the world.

Since 1973 the world economy has been painfully adjusting to an economic crisis triggered by an unprecedented increase in the price of oil, a commodity that has become the life-blood of modern economies. The result has been a recession out of which we are just beginning to move. It is not a recession which stemmed from any policy decisions of any of the major western trading nations. And recession is not the *only* 'invisible' that we are obliged to import whether we like it or not. Technological change is another: whether its consequences are adverse or beneficial is at the heart of the question being discussed.

Microelectronics, a key area of technological change much in the news recently, has tended to be depicted as the greatest threat to employment since the Wall Street crash. Other concerns in the past (for example, with pollution of the atmosphere and the seas) have led to changes in public policy, and also to changes in private behaviour. Damage caused to the environment by current policies, methods of production, and industrial waste processes was recognised, whereupon appropriate legislation (eg the Clean Air Act) and other measures were adopted.

Public concern of this sort, dismissed by some as an intellectual fad, is no bad thing. This is true in the field of microelectronics. (It is worth noting that environmental issues and microelectronics are not entirely unconnected: microprocessors should help to save raw materials, especially the fossil fuels; and should help the American motor industry to achieve the current targets for exhaust emission.) Examples can be given of major technological advances which have had profound effects on all our lives. The first is the appearance of plastics. This is a good example of change which had few obvious implications for employment beyond the actual production of the plastics themselves when first introduced. But their versatility was such that there was virtually no end to the products that did not have to take account of them. Perhaps the most profound effect upon employment was in the economic growth they made possible as a result of their relatively low cost.

Another example is the computer revolution itself. Here a highly sophisticated new technology had direct and obvious manpower implications. Computers could do things which were traditionally performed by people, and the direst predictions were made about potential effects on employment. These original predictions now seem to have been unduly pessimistic, but some of the reasons why the pessimists were proved wrong are worth considering.

One is undoubtedly that the traditional mainframe computers and their associated input and output devices represented very major investments. As we move towards more capital-intensive production processes, we see a change in the pattern of employment. More people are employed in fulfilling investment plans as fewer people are employed in actually controlling the production processes.

If one could draw a graph of the effect of a major factory investment decision, the employment implications of that decision shown on the graph would move very rapidly upwards through the work in the design office and the drawing office to the point of production of the machinery for the new modern factory. The erection upon site would involve the employment of many thousands of people, but on the day that the plant came on-stream, the labour required to operate the plant would drop to something which would be a very small percentage of the maximum employment effect of the decision. This is a very different picture from that of the investment scene in the last part of the last century or the early part of this century. At that time, when the production equipment was relatively crude, the labour requirement was massive.

Subsequent developments have brought about a change in the pattern of employment but we must not confuse the change in the pattern with a change in absolute levels: the two are not the same. So predictions that have often accompanied the introduction of new processes have often been unduly pessimistic.

Technological developments do not take place overnight. There has often been ample time in the past to adjust within the economy to new technologies. This does not mean that there will be ample time in the future, and we have to consider whether the time-scale and the pace of change is itself accelerating at such a rate as to require us to respond in a different way.

Computers have also released resources by performing almost instantaneously, routine jobs which required an immense clerical effort. Many of the people released from clerical chores were themselves trained into computer operating skills. The result, as more computer applications become possible, was an increase in service rather than an increase in jobs.

There are many examples where service appears to have suffered. Sometimes, when contacting some organisation to request information, we are told, "Oh – we cannot provide you with that now because we are on the computer." This suggests that some people have not fully understood the computer process: it should always increase the service provision and the control quality, never diminish them. If service or quality are adversely affected, there can be implications for employment.

There is no necessary link between technological advance and unemployment. The past five years have seen tremendous technological change, and not only technological change arising out of computer development. But the numbers in employment now are in fact greater than those of five years ago, and this in a period of slump. On the latest available figures (March 1978), there were 22,047,000 people employed in the UK, and in March 1973, 22,106,000. This small change reflects upon why we have higher unemployment – the change in population age range and the very much greater number of people seeking jobs. However, the numbers of people in employment now are very similar to those in employment five years ago, despite the fact that this period has seen the worst economic recession since the Second World War.

The interesting thing about microtechnology is that it possesses many of the features of both of the examples of technological change discussed above. Like plastics, there is almost no end to the applications of the new technology that can be foreseen and microelectronics offers cost advantages over products or systems it is likely to replace. Microprocessors are immensely cheaper than conventional computers, and also cheaper than the equivalent electromechanical control systems.

Even where the microelectronically-based products are more expensive than the products that they are likely to replace, for example the cost of a word processor as compared with a typewriter, the productivity gains of the microprocessor or the microcontrolled process justify the investment.

As with computers, microelectronic technology can often replace people. Why, in such circumstances, should the government promote applications of it? If a technology offers significant competitive advantages, then we either adopt it or do not compete at all. If our competitors boost productivity and reduce costs by employing new techniques, then, if we wish to maintain employment and improve our living standards, we have no option. We cannot use an outdated labour-intensive method to sustain employment. Even if we kept labour costs low by paying low wages, we would not be able to offset the enormous production advantage conferred by the latest technologies. In the most capital-intensive forms of production, the labour cost for running the on-stream process is insignificant. No savings in labour costs can offset the cost of using an outdated process.

The government's approach to the challenge of this new technology is threefold: a first line of attack is that this is too important a technology for us to leave the development to our industrial competitors. The National Enterprise Board, INMOS venture, and the Department of Industry programmes designed to stimulate the existing British microelectronic industry, indicate the government's intention that we take full advantage of the employment potential in this area. The government also recognises that the way in which the technology will make itself most felt is not so much by what happens in the electronics industry itself, as in what use is made of its products elsewhere in our economy. The Department of Industry has therefore embarked upon a programme designed to help industry in the identification of areas where microelectronics application can lead to very well worthwhile efficiency gains, and remove obstacles from the making of this application.

A most remarkable recent example of this was where Bowater Scotts in Barrow had the first run on a de-inking process. The actual chemical process and the material handling aspect of it represented no dramatic improvement on the general technology of de-inking. What was remarkable was that, with the new electronic control process, the whole thing could be run by one person.

This relates also to the environmental process, because the first batch of paper they put through for de-inking consisted of a bundle of computer printouts, so to some extent it was a case of one computer technology, or one electronic technology, being aided by another. Certainly both make a very considerable contribution towards resolving the environmental problem of knocking down trees and using a lot of other very valuable material in order to create paper.

A potential obstacle to developing the use of the technology in a way which aids employment is shortage of manpower in the necessary knowledge and skills. One of the most demanding aspects in the development of of manpower policy for the unions and the government is this continued skill shortage at a time of intolerably high unemployment. The government and the Manpower Services Commission are very heavily engaged in working out ways of meeting the training and the retraining requirements which are thrown up by the development of new technologies generally, and this technology in particular.

The third aspect of the government's approach is less immediately practical, but nonetheless vital. The Prime Minister has asked the Central Policy Review staff to look at the potential social and economic effects of microelectronic technology. They will be looking to the Department of Employment for advice as to manpower and employment effects. There is now a small group within the Unit for Manpower Studies to study and report upon potential effects of the technology on jobs, skills and employment patterns.

Of all the potential effects on manpower of microelectronic technology the most urgent is undoubtedly this: which sectors of the British economy are most vulnerable to competition through their failure to keep abreast of new technology? There is no certainty about job loss if we do apply microelectronic technology. There is an absolute certainty about job loss if we do not. It is not possible to give firm forecasts where microelectronics technology will first begin to make a major impact or what the effect on jobs will be.

In telecommunications we already have a very good example of people feeling the impact, not only in the operation of systems (known only too well by the POEU) but in the manufacturing area.Three major firms who employed a lot of people in the manufacture of Strowger and Crossbar equipment for our telephone exchanges, are now switching to the TX systems, at a time when the TX systems can be produced with very much less labour. This is a dramatic example of where one not only has fewer people employed in the actual operation as a result of microelectronic technology, but fewer engaged in the production of the equipment.

The car industry is also important from the point of view of microelectronics applications. Here, and in other engineering industries, a distinction has to be made between the impact of microelectronics on components and the impact upon the production line. With components there will be a whole host of microelectronic devices replacing existing ranges of control and instrumentation, both in the means of production, and in the car itself. In the car, microelectronics will play a part in processing and control in such areas as ignition, fuel control, dashboard instruments and exhaust emission control.

The technology will make possible new ranges of instruments and driving aids which up to now have offered no employment potential: microprocessed route-finding and routeing are now feasible, and they have no equivalents within our existing technology. So there is potential for employment of a new kind. It will not be enough simply to note all the existing control and instrumentation systems which will have micro-electronic equivalents, and to conclude that the employment effects will therefore be negligible. It is also going to be necessary to make an assessment of the labour force mix that will be necessary to produce a new range of systems as compared with the old. We shall have to ask the questions about what the material content of these new systems will be, and then trace that back through the production process to the implications for supplies of materials.

The whole business of assessing impact is an extremely complex one. It runs right through from the point of material supply to the very nature and design of the new product.

Quite clearly we can foresee microelectronics making an impact upon car production lines. Microprocessor-controlled welding and paint-spraying machines are already a reality, and it would be foolish to pretend that they could have other than a negative effect upon the number of people employed in the production line.

It is surely worth noting that there are few jobs more unpleasant and hazardous to health than paint spraying. So if a computer can take over the job of paint spraying then there is an aspect of that which we can welcome wholeheartedly. It is another linkage between microelectronics and environmental health and safety issues.

Total employment in this country and in other economies heavily dependent upon manufacture, is far more a function of total demand for a given product or total output of a product, than it is of the technology employed to produce that product. Efficiency, high productivity, is usually generative of higher demand. So it would be wrong to suppose that the loss of individual production-line jobs will necessarily mean overall loss of employment. This applies across the board and not just to the car industry. It is certainly the case that the number of cars that can be produced and purchased has not fallen as the job has become more capital-intensive; it has increased. The Model T Ford, an example of the best manufacturing technology of its day, was produced by far too labour-intensive a process. This rendered it too expensive to be bought by the vast majority of people. Today's car (and its components), produced by a less labour-intensive process, is usable by a far greater proportion of the population.

In the process industries the major impact of microelectronic technology is more likely to be qualitative. There will be employment effects but the main effect will be to replace existing ranges of control and monitoring devices with better and cheaper devices. Existing control and monitoring devices in process industries have already replaced a great deal of labour. It would certainly be true to say that microelectronic technology can do no worse in employment terms than continue an existing trend. It will not originate the trend, and it will not lead to any horrifying sudden new change which in itself will create mass unemployment.

Much discussion in the media has tended to concentrate on the office work area as the place in which it is most likely to have a devastating effect upon the demand for labour. It would be very worrying indeed if some of the predictions were to materialise, because the trend in advanced industrial countries and in particular in our own country since the war, has been increasingly for the service sector to provide more jobs as the manufacturing sector has become more capital-intensive and provides fewer. In fact the Manpower Services Commission, in their first full survey of the change in the pattern of employment in the UK, referred to a 10-year period immediately prior to the present slump, when the number of people employed in manufacturing fell by one million and the number of people employed in servicing increased by one million. More people were employed in schools, in hospitals, in the provision of public services. Therefore, if the effect of microelectronics was only to stabilise the number required to be employed in services, let alone reduce them, that would be a very worrying thing in employment manpower policy terms. It would have very serious complications for us and the political decisions which we are going to have to take on manpower policies.

The past experience of the computer revolution tends to suggest that the pessimists overestimate the speed with which it takes place, and of course it would be wrong to regard office work and the service sector as being absolutely synonymous. There is a great deal of office work in the manufacturing sector. Nevertheless, office work does represent a very significant proportion of total employment in the service sector.

The widespread use of computers in this area is already with us, in fields such as banking, insurance and other financial sectors. We are still a long way from the totally electronic and paperless office. What is likely over the next five years or so, is a more widespread employment of word processing equipment of one sort or another. Some private organisations have already claimed some very dramatic results for word processors. However, the needs of organisations vary greatly. A commercial firm whose approach to marketing involves issuing a large number of identical but apparently personalised letters would, for instance, have a need which is not matched by government departments.

Firms marketing word processors might also be expected to take every opportunity to utilise them. The government have been trying to use word processors in various government departments. Our experience is that very significant productivity gains can be made in areas for which the word processor is especially suited (such as production of lengthy documents which go through a great many drafts). However, while they can be very valuable in reducing tedious and repetitive retyping and proof-reading, word processors are more likely to help overcome a shortage of typists than to cause redundancies among civil service typists. It is likely that experience in the private sector will be similar to the experience of the civil service in the use of word processors over the next five years.

Even in the area of office work, where there are some positive aspects to the employment effects of using microtechnology, the development is a slow and on-going one. In the economy as a whole, the microelectronic revolution is going to cause an enormous increase in the demand for people with computer-related skills. Part of this increase in demand will be for very highly qualified specialists, but perhaps the larger part of the demand is going to be for office workers with more technical skills than currently required. These skills could be acquired, given any reasonable training programme by existing office workers.

The skills will be required to handle the increased capacity, to manipulate information, and to manipulate it in new ways. There is no reason why such demand may not be met by retraining people who currently fear the loss of their jobs as a result of microtechnology. We are beginning to see a very interesting phenomenon in office employment in parts of the United States, where in some areas they are getting much closer to the fully electronic office than we have done in this country. There they have found that, as the complexity of word processing equipment increases, more machines achieve their optimum performance only when linked and worked in conjunction with other machines. So the office worker needs to develop more technical skill.

One of the effects of this in America has been to break down traditional barriers between those involved in doing routine jobs in the offices and those involved in management or in more demanding information processing work.

It is worth noting that we inevitably look at new technology in a some-what timid way when we are in a period of recession. We might look at it differently if we were in a period of expansion.

Economists generally tend to the view that growth in productivity is invariably associated with growth in employment. If we believe that in the case of microelectronic technology this relationship is bound to be broken, then perhaps we have been living for too long with too high a level of unemployment. The productivity gains that microelectronic technology can bring, can help economies out of a recession and restore the pattern of fast economic growth that characterised the performance of many economies throughout the 1950s and 1960s.

It is not possible totally to isolate the effect of microelectronic technology from a whole series of technology developments which in cumulative effect are having a massive impact on the number of jobs required to achieve a given industrial performance, given output levels.

The total effect of capital-intensive development on employment is enormous, and particularly in a period of recession. Nor can we guarantee that we will be able to expand state services to provide the additional jobs for those displaced. Even if we could mount the training services that were needed, there is justification for concern at this on-going process. The process is already happening, and the use of the latest technology may cause it to grow and advance. It may be difficult to cope with, given our present instruments of intervention and our present practices in the employment field. Most people assume that they will train within the first four or five years of leaving school to acquire a particular skill to enable them to earn their bread and butter for the rest of their lives.

It does challenge us to most enormous changes. The Luddites were not wrong to fear the introduction of a new technology. They were right to be concerned about it. They were right in their supposition that when a new manufacturing method came about it would have an impact on their ability to earn their living, that it might face them with unemployment with terrible drops in living standards.

The difference between the introduction of new technology then and the new technology now is not in its impact upon the nature of employment. The difference is that now we have democratic representation in the political field. We have developed a trade union movement in this country. We are challenged by the accelerating pace of technology to advance industrial democracy, to advance political analysis and understanding and to formulate policies by which we can exploit technology in the interest of the majority of the people.

# 3 Discussion

## Questions to Rt Hon Albert Booth

*Mr J Cooke:* As we change our technology people become more and more skilled in various new subjects. We then have difficulty keeping them in this country, because in the US they can earn $2\frac{1}{2}$ times what they can here. In Germany and other countries they can earn perhaps even more than that: with an international combine like Ford Motor Company, this becomes immediately apparent to all our people.

The Common Market encourages the mobility of labour, which makes it more likely that we will lose our people. The problem is particularly acute in specific areas – draughtsmen, systems analysts, etc. How do we reconcile the problem of keeping these skills in this country with the policy of pay restraint which reduces the flexibility of trades unions and management? The artificial methods being used to skirt round this problem – for instance, British Leyland people coming to Fords, and Ford people going to British Leyland – are only adding to the problem. Can the government include in its pay policies the flexibility required in the complex business world?

*Mr L Clyne:* The way in which the new technology develops has been discussed. The high initial labour cost involved in development has been contrasted with the small labour force required in production. The introduction of word processors for example, as at Logica, changes the way in which people are involved with the technology. There are now few regular permanent typists and a shift system to get the maximum productivity out of the capital involved.

We have seen similar effects with computers themselves, with most operators also working the shift system. This suggests that the technology is determining how people work and not the other way round. Comments would be welcome on this aspect of the problem.

*Mr E Lancashire:* The new technology is going to place extreme demands on people's intellect and the ability to cope.

On the one hand, we have in industry an ever-growing older set of technicians. As people get older it is more difficult to grasp the new methods, particularly if they see that at the end of it their jobs are going to change markedly or even disappear.

On the other hand, the schools in the last eight years have not been able to focus pupils and school leavers into jobs where they can learn a manual or technical trade. Often they have taken mundane jobs or been forced into unemployment.

There is also the attitude of skilled engineering workers on the shop floor. Skilled NC machinists, for example, having accepted the NC tapes in the initial stages, are now demanding more control over the technology, to develop technical skills. Draughtsmen and technicians see this as a threat to their position. Comments about these problems would be welcome.

*Rt Hon Albert Booth:* The question of how we keep people in this country, given that we can develop high levels of skill in great demand during the introduction of new technology, really demands a twofold answer. Whether people remain in this country is not merely a question of how much they are paid relative to their counterparts in other countries. It is interesting to talk to shipyard workers who have returned from Germany or to aircraft designers or medical specialists who have decided to return from the States. Some of them are concerned about the whole quality of life and how the increased wealth produced by new technology can be used to provide better social services.

Another consideration derives from political beliefs. It is not right that the only thing that should control the relative income of a person is the current demand for a particular skill: it would mean, for example, that the riveter for whom there was no demand when welding took over, should have had a wage of one tenth of that of the man who could train to become a welder. Part of the social cost of embracing new technologies has to be the cost of training people whose skills are displaced, and of compensating them to a degree for loss of earning capacity.

Pay policy has become more flexible over the past few years. It began with a rigid policy of £6 for everyone under £8500 p.a., and nothing for those over (with the exception of equal pay claims). Then a whole series of different adjustments were introduced – pension adjustments, fair wages claims, schedule II claims, productivity arrangements, etc.

In the 10% round, in the phase 3, the majority of negotiators faced with an option of giving some 8% and some 12% and resolving and changing differentials, and paying in accordance with changes of structure within firms, rejected it. The majority said that 10% is all we can get against the present cost of living and the present background, so we will have it equally all round.

We must work in greater flexibility. Major restructuring or major changes in job pattern have to be related to income. There is flexibility for this, providing that the increase in demand is compatible with the increase in output. To ignore this would jeopardise the improved balance of payments situation, our stronger currency, greater foreign reserves and so on.

The shift system being introduced for workers as a result of new technology is a very serious social question. The new technology releases some people from shift work and brings other people into shift work who have not faced it before. Because there will be fewer people engaged in process control in manufacturing there will be fewer people engaged in shift work in that particular area. In other areas, particularly running some of the higher-powered computers in order to justify the cost, there will be people on shift work for the first time.

The question is: how do we meet this in social terms? How do we provide facilities for people who are on shift work with facilities to do things in hours outside work? That can be tackled through a whole series of local authority arrangements, and regional council arrangements. What we have not tackled in the majority of industries is how to compensate an individual for the change of work pattern in terms,of his overall working life. Is it reasonable to ask some people to spend a part of their working life at nights and resting during the day, at the same time giving them other facilities, a higher rate of pay and a night-shift premium? Compensations we are going to have to develop should also be in terms of retirement age, longer holidays, sabbatical time and so on. Even on that basis it will still be a difficult choice.

At United Biscuits in London the shop stewards had among themselves agreed the high-shift premium arrangement of operating the most advanced conputer-controlled biscuit-making process in this country. A computer does the job of determining the content that is fed into a cooking process. This is a very advanced use. It was decided that those who worked the night shift – and there should be an option to work it – should receive one third more per hour than those who worked the two day shifts. What they found in practice was that 80% of those who opted to do night shift were immigrants, people who had come to this country within the last 10 years or so. Most people who had lived in this country for the whole of their lives opted to take a wage which was three-quarters of what they could have got on night shift, in order that they could maintain their existing social patterns. There has to be a social pattern compensation as well as pay compensation.

With regard to school leavers, special provision will have to be made over the next four years. We do not have a training capacity which is sufficiently flexible to allow for another 150,000 people to come into apprenticeships and other vocational training. We will change that by use of the opportunities programme. We also need to have more flexible age on entry into all sorts of vocational training. Where the older worker faces the prospect of his skill becoming redundant, one has to decide how far one can meet his particular position by retraining. It takes some older workers longer to retrain than younger workers, but we have to develop a total new approach to education. The idea that education is something that switches off when the majority of people are 16 is a patent nonsense in terms of a modern rapidly changing society. We must see education as an on-going process, and the right to train and update and study in a number of subjects, some of which will be totally unrelated to work must be part of the future which a modern high technology society will offer. The question of enabling people who were doing highly skilled work on machines to move over into control of the technical input is a matter to be thrashed out within the trade union movement. It is not particularly helpful for any government minister, including one from the Department of Employment, to say that it is better that existing people in drawing offices or design offices should stand aside and take into their ranks people to control technical processes, who have previously been engaged in turning handles on machines.

The challenge cuts across the traditional demarcations. It is not only in the engineering factory, where the lathe operator is faced with the numerical control of his machine – look at the printing industry! It is the compositor faced with the proposition that all of his skill, built up over two centuries, is going to be set aside by a computer which can set the front page of a newspaper in 90 seconds, taking the input of a typewriter and appropriate instructions.

This question throws up a challenge for the trade union movement to meet much more the conflict between craft (and sectional) interests and total industrial interests.

*Mr A Marshall:*  In recent years, Plessey Telecommunications have enjoyed a considerable export market. This is now diminishing. You cannot sell communications to the developed world because they have got their own companies supplying that need. In the third world, people want to buy know-how. They do not really want to buy hardware. They want us to set up an operation where they can manufacture, take on the maintenance, maintain their own design and develop the system for their particular country. In the future we will not protect jobs for the man on the automatic lathe in the press shop or in the wiring shop, but we will only create jobs which sell know-how. It is difficult to see how society, as presently organised, could cope with such requirements.

*Mr R Cooper:* GEC has recently produced an annual report and in it the Assistant Managing Director says that the overwhelming need is for physicists, mathematicians, electronic engineers, mechanical engineers, computer engineers, programmers, and to a lesser extent designers, draughtsmen and test engineers. Which service industries will take on the redundant lathe operator? And in view of the fact that it takes perhaps 10 years to produce a good physicist/mathematician, how will we actually convert the manufacturing industry labour force into the happy service industry force?

*Mr P M Luck:* The aviation industry and most of the high technology industries in this country today are moving towards a higher integration of new technologies, not only microelectronics, computers and the like, but also new technologies which will do away with the traditional methods of manufacture. We have seen the advent of computer-aided design, computer-aided manufacture, and the processing of masses of paperwork. They have been installed one at a time. The only thing now that stops the reduction in employment and the holding of labour is the interface between the three systems. We are fast approaching that point in time those interfaces will no longer be required. What are we going to do about the unemployment that will result?

*Mr J Cooke:* It is worth making a comment about the international automotive industry regarding design and development, including the use of computers in this area.

We do benefit without a doubt from the international-combine approach within the automotive sphere in Ford Motor Company, as can be seen by its success in many aspects. But with those benefits, both in terms of scale and capital etc, and know-how from the States, there have come a lot of problems, and we are torn in the trade union movement. This is particularly on the design and development side, rather than on the manufacturing side.

We need to co-operate more closely with our German counterparts – because they are really part of Ford of Europe – but there are also problems of centralisation in America. Massive computers, involving high capital cost, are necessary to deal with the number-crunching aspect. Total car design and development is being focussed in America. There are fringe benefits – sales and implementation of America-based designs – but there is concern about centralisation.

The British government guaranteed that design and research and development would stay in Britain when Ford Britain was taken over by Ford America. In fact there is now total centralisation in the States. The computers and communications that can be internationally achieved by the satellite links make it much more profitable to operate on a world basis.

We are now operating really on a world car basis. The Escort, Cortina, etc, will be on this basis, with some modifications. In our industry, on the development and design side, there will be a rundown on the number of people required because of centralisation in the States. Perhaps people will recognise the need for a world-wide approach to things and a sharing out of labour in the various countries; or perhaps we will centralise in those Western countries that have the power to maintain such an arrangement.

*Rt Hon Albert Booth:* There will be a number of areas in under-developed and developing countries where they will be looking for the purchase of know-how, rather than the purchase of the manufactured product. For many of these countries, the decision as to whether to buy the know-how and set up their own manufacturing plant, or whether to buy the product, will depend only partially on the nature of the technology. Clearly, some of the less sophisticated microelectronics equipment is such that it can be produced by a labour force, the majority of whom can be trained in a process of about six months, and there are a relatively small number who have a much higher degree of skill and knowledge. It is a feasible process for some of the less sophisticated businesses, but it is unrealistic to train people and to set up manufacturing facilities for some of the most advanced new products.

That is only one consideration. Another is the way we trade with them, and this will be one of the problems for the EEC. If advanced Western countries are prepared – or forced – to pay a proper price for primary products (food and raw materials), it is sensible and fair to pay them in terms of providing the advanced sophisticated equipment which we can make very well.

Some agreement should be developed within the EEC to help us to reach a bilateral or a multilateral arrangement with the under-developed countries to help them buy some of the products of our advanced industries with the raw materials that they have to sell, rather than forcing them into a position where they have the maximum incentive to industrialise. There is a great danger that if we use the government cartel power, inherent in the EEC to depress the prices of those who have to sell into EEC their primary produce, they are going to tighten their belts and go through an almost Stalinist period, saying that no matter what it costs they will develop their own manufacturing industry, because the manufacturing industry nations of the world are the "haves", and those who produce the primary produce are the "have nots". This raises wider political factors. However, it is right to sell know-how in certain cases, whether this relates to manufacturing or to training techniques.

Many displaced people – for example – those hit by the changeover from the electromechanical to the electronic in telecommunications – will work in service areas. The advanced technician will be needed in the medical service of the future. Medicine will need a great number of technicians using a lot of sophisticated equipment, as will teaching and other services. It is a precondition that the manufacturing sector creates the wealth to finance the non-saleable public services.

With regard to centralisation (the Ford example is a good one), this question is also being overtaken by the technology. The silicon chip has dramatically reduced the size of computer equipment. Cost and weight are related, even when you are moving from very heavy outdated equipment to very modern sophisticated equipment. As computing devices become smaller and cheaper, it becomes increasingly feasible to use them as design aids in many more centres of production.

The first step in a new microtechnology involves a very expensive layout of very high capital investment (for example, the setting up of INMOS through NEB is a very expensive business) but that leads on, very rapidly in some cases, to a product which is very much less expensive. That this has been hidden by high rates of inflation over the past few years should not blind us to the underlying development.

The electronic watch could not be produced 10 years ago as it is today. We should consider how far decisions to vest design in particular places are in fact controlled by the cost and availability of computer aids to design. If this is a major factor, then it certainly has ramifications for all governments who want to intervene in economies in countries where much of the manufacturing is handled by multinational companies. We have not yet developed instruments of intergovernmental co-operation which do more than insubstantially influence. We have not yet developed a form of control of the multinational company which throws up the biggest threat in this area.

*Mr J Rowan:* The bosses have not changed since the time when the Luddites gave their response to the advanced technology of their day. The bosses response is something like this:

"Look, we don't give a damn that to get energy, people are required to work in damp, dirty, dangerous holes in the ground, or that to provide transport for masses more now than when Henry Ford produced his T Model, people have to work in assembly lines and grind their way down the line to the psychiatric unit at the end. We are not concerned about easing these things, unless in easing them and introducing technology to ease them, the primary consideration is that we make a profit."

It is as true now as it was then. It is as true today in Chrysler, about to be bought over by Peugeot, as it is in BL Cars (where there is supposed to be some national interest at stake and where the bosses assume something more than the profit motive).

The interface problem, raised earlier, is very important. This is not only the interface between varying levels of skilled or deskilled persons, it relates much more to the social and political consciousness which the trade unions have engendered amongst their members of the awareness of people of the deskilling of their jobs, and of the inevitable consequence of that deskilling.

At a presentation by BL Cars, they outlined the basic requirements of their reorganisation to us. The PSF Company – that is Pressed Steel Fisher – has as one of its primary objectives "to maintain technological leadership in, for example, computer-aided design, pressed steel manufacture and the production process." However, internationally they are concentrating their areas of necessary skill in a global sense to suit the global market requirements of the multinationals who, in a few years' time, will probably produce two major companies in Japan producing automobiles, two in the United States and two in Europe. Also, in Cowley there is an advanced design centre, a styling centre, which is producing work which hundreds and hundreds of members produced some years ago.

At the University of Manchester there is an engine test bed for the O-Series engine, perhaps one of their biggest successes in Leyland so far, which no longer has test engineers around it. It has these funny little chips that not only run the engine at infinitely-variable performance levels, that not only record all of its performance, but begin to postulate through the use of computers and advanced technology, new parameters, new concepts of design for the development of that engine and indeed for future engines. So the scores of highly-skilled jobs that were created only 10 or 15 or 20 years ago are now being boiled down into bits of technology.

At Llanelli Radiators, they have a spark erosion machine which is linked to a computer, which in turn is linked to a computer which is in Canada, which in turn is linked to a computer in Switzerland. The spark erosion machine was developed 25 or 30 years ago in the heartlands of Russia by a scientist to take out punches that had broken. Today it is a sophisticated preproduction prototype and production tool, capable of working within three microns. It is capable not only of reproducing to that level of tolerance, prototypes and tools, but indeed is the harbinger of an ability to do something much more – to transmit information on a previously unknown scale.

This is very important. At the beginning of the year it was indicated when Michael Edwards took over British Leyland, that he had prepared the ground to bring in a totally designed car from outside the United Kingdom. This immediately struck at the hearts of our 5000 members in BL Cars and you can understand their reaction.

They immediately said, "Right, nobody will handle one single design, one single volume of calculation, the truck loads of paperwork necessary to conceive, engineer and produce a car." Already today the technology is available to shortcircuit our 5000 members in the inevitably Luddite reaction to developments which impinge on their job security. All you need is the introductory code number to a computer bank. You dial the number. You plug in your telephone line, and the information flows. That is happening in Ford. It is happening in Chrysler. It is happening in GM. It is happening in Leyland.

The social implications of these developments are not being recognised, even in a company as socially responsible as BL Cars. The profit motive is still the primary motivating force. So when it opens a new plant at Rover Solihull with seven computers controlling the three floor paint sprays, controlling the automated pallets into the assembly line – the consequence is to upset the social pattern of people's lives. There is increasing emphasis on the need for shift work.

The decline – to use Leyland again as an example – in numbers of engineers envisaged over the next seven years is dramatic. That is not because they are not requiring all the skill, expertise and indeed the increased numbers of engineers and technologists today. This is because of the implications of the transferability and the availability of global car information in a global sense to meet a global strategy of these global internationals.

It is important that we recognise that the problems are not Chrysler problems, or Ford problems, or Leyland problems, or Lucas problems, but are the social/political problems that we have in this country.

*Mr E Lancashire:* The question relating to the different skills of the skilled man and the technical man has not been answered. It is important that the government, and particularly the Manpower Services Commission, be aware of this problem.

In 1971 there was a tremendous cutback, at Rolls Royce in Derby, of highly qualified people. One or two of them were able to go into technical colleges to train to be teachers, but because of the government cutback in public spending fewer teachers are required, and this also affects people in the National Health Service. We have found that some of these people who did train to be teachers, who did get a job, are now no longer employed as teachers, because they are surplus, and they have been persuaded by one means or another to find different jobs. Some indeed have come back into the aricraft industry.

There has been a miserable failure of government with regard to employ-ment and engineering skills. It is said that the manufacturing industries produce the wealth, but there is evidence of a massive move of employment into the services rather than into manufacturing. In Derby, for example, many people in the engineering industry are advising their sons and daughters to keep out of it, to seek a different sort of employment.

The profit motive is not ill-conceived, but there is a new breed in charge of industry, who have no humanity, no soul. There has been a failure over the past eight years to make sure there was employment for people, that there were people trained and paid adequately. Computing will cause further unemployment in the aircraft industry. In Rolls Royce in Derby the work-force is ever growing older: there are 10 or 12 men (out of 270) below the age of 40 in the design office, and in seven years' time a third of that office will have retired. The government should look carefully at these developments and bear its responsibility towards the unemployed people.

*Ms D McMillan:* GEC have got a set-up which they seem to be implementing throughout their companies. At Trafford Park we have got computers which are going into the specification areas. We have got machines now which are going into the draughting areas, and we have got NC tapes. We can see that with this kind of thing we will get the interface automated and the whole thing will go through from one process to another. It is no accident that the latest Weinstock report did actually contain the demand for computer and allied technological skills and people. One of the things that concerned us among these reports was the movement towards central data banks, etc. This is a similar process to the development of the universal car discussed earlier.

It has not been emphasised that the reduced cost of computers will lead to an accelerating rate of use. The fears expressed a few years ago were not wrong. It is just that the economic recession has delayed developments. The USA and other countries have built up their skills and knowledge in this area and to some extent we are cashing in.

The work force at GEC, Trafford Park, has an average age of about 50. New people have been taken in for training in the advanced skills.

It has been suggested that displaced people will move into the services. In fact there are no plans to increase the services. One report says that teachers will be cut over the next 10 years by 100,000. This is the kind of thing we are looking at all over the place.

We should be grateful to the media for programmes such as "Now the Chips are Down", because that is getting through to some of the members of the trade union movement – ordinary working people who are suddenly realising what this means, the kinds of fears and problems and questions that responsible trade unionists have been aware of for some time but cannot get through. This is one place where the media have actually given something to our members.

Over the last 12 months we have been facing a very sustained stand by the CBI on no change in the social pattern. We have also seen, each and every day, redundancies and closures. The latest one this week was somewhere around 400 people at Massey Ferguson. That was one of the things that was reported and it has been going on up and down the country. We are all aware of places like Liverpool and so on. We do need a government with some kind of social responsibility.

*Rt Hon Albert Booth:* With allocation of work the best way forward is by inter-union agreement. It is easy to understand the attitude of Engineering Section members who expect to be trained in the newer processes that are displacing them as machine operators. Similarly, NGA members have a claim to be trained to operate the computer which takes over from the skill of the compositor. It is to be hoped that these questions will be solved within the ranks of the trade union movement.

It is true that new technology has affected the employment rolls at British Leyland. There are also other factors. British Leyland has lost a substantial part of the British market to people who have employed more advanced technologies more effectively. If British Leyland had used the best technologists that are available in this country as effectively as they could be used, it might have won a bigger share of the world market, as well as the British market, instead of contributing to a situation in which more than half of the cars purchased in this country in a year are purchased from abroad.

It has been suggested that we can organise employment in services for those people who are displaced by the introduction of new technologies in manufacturing industry. However, we will only be able to employ in services people who will be displaced by modern technology in manufacturing industry, if we shape the instruments which can ensure that a large measure of the wealth created by that manufacturing industry is available for the expenditure on services.

This is a question which is having to be answered around the Cabinet table year by year in public expenditure exercises. Social spending was squeezed at the end of 1976. Shirley Williams was not lacking in concern for maintaining the employment of teachers. David Ennals was not lacking in concern for sustaining employment in hospitals. The terrifying decision which we had to make was: were we going to stop expenditure in support of industry in order to sustain expenditure in the social field. The situation was not determined within parameters of a British Cabinet's making, but within parameters which were largely the making of the IMF, which said to a British Cabinet, "You cannot go on borrowing money on the scale you want to borrow it, to fund an expansion of your public services. We will lay a condition upon you, that the amount that you can borrow will be determined by the sum of your public sector borrowing requirements and your balance of payments deficit." In other words the proposition that they put to us was, "You can spend more on your public services, if you can do something to remove your balance of payments deficit." That is what they said.

Or they put it the other way round as well, if you like. They said, "If you cut your public services, you can have a bigger balance of payments deficit and still borrow the money." That was a totally ludicrous proposition. How are we going to get out of a world recession if the action of the IMF is such that countries which are prepared to run deficits in order to sustain and build up public services are going to be prevented from doing so, while they operate in a way in which they can take over the services and provide a market for companies capable of making services?

That is what actually happened. That is the way that the decisions have to be made, and so it would not have been in the interests of employment of our members, or employment of people in the public services, had we said that we must expand our public services even within these world conditions which we now face and therefore we are not going to make available money to NEB to sustain British Leyland. We are not going to make money available to sustain our machine tool industry or to save our foundries or for an intervention fund to save our shipbuilding industry.

That is the way that the decision is taken. The British government must have at its command a share of the wealth that can be created by organising the support for a sensible investment policy within the manufacturing sector. In other words we will pay a price now in terms of how far we can expand our public services in order that our industry can make intelligent use of the best technologies to create the wealth that we need in this country.

The trade unions should play a bigger part in shaping those policies, those corporate decisions, in order to see that two things happen: one is that public support is used in the most intelligent way, so that we do get the best possible output, so that we do diversify as far as we can in order to maintain employment at the highest possible levels that we can. And secondly, we should ensure that the amount of public support is not only no higher than it has to be, but that the time is most quickly achieved, when industry, instead of requiring public support, is making an essential contribution to the public coffers, in order that the services can be expanded, which will not only provide employment for people displaced, but will raise our general living standards and our level of social services in this country.

# 4   The view from Western Europe

**German Metalworkers**

*Mr K Mehrens:* The problems in Germany are similar to those in the UK. Computer industries and electronics are certainly growing industries in Germany as well. We have had growth rates of from 12 to 15% in recent years, and we have also a growth in employment, which is smaller of course, but which is between 3 and 5%. Much more important in our view is the effect on other industries for which we have some examples. These effects are mainly negative and sometimes they are disastrous for employment.

Our position in relation to these problems is very difficult. On the one hand, we are interested in the development of productivity and of new products which can make our lives easier. Certainly in our country lots of problems remain to be solved and many examples could be found where our workers could use their skills with a highly positive effect for society. This is valid for our country, and it is even more valid if we take the developing countries into consideration.

On the other hand, technological progress places us in a situation where even the already existing employment problems are almost insuperable. I do not want to go into details of describing the dangers and the possibilities of microprocessors, but let me summarise the strategies which our union has adopted or supported to meet the serious employment problems resulting from this development.

The strategies can be divided into three areas. One is the overall national economic policy. Another is the structural policy concerning regions on the one hand and sectors and industries on the other hand. Thirdly and lastly, are our bargaining policies.

On average, German industry works at about 80% of its capacity and that means that jobs do exist in our industry, but there are no people doing the jobs. The result of this is an unemployment figure of more than one million people for the fourth year now, and we think that the main reason for this is a lack of overall demand. So the first point in our strategy is that we support the strengthening of overall demand. A low-wage policy is not an adequate way to reach this goal.

The second point is an effective structural policy. For years all German unions have developed a detailed box of tools for such a policy, but the government is very hesitant to apply these tools. They rely, much more than in England, on the forces of free-market dynamics.

New technologies are now menacing whole industries both in the quality and quantity of work. The first example we had was the watch industry, the second could be the machine-tool industry. There is an increasing need to take effective measures in the field of structural policy. We have to interpret market forecasts accurately. We feel that in this field a sectional approach is not sufficient. Nowadays almost every sectional crisis is also a regional crisis, so these analyses also have to be done on a regional basis.

Secondly, we have to support the location of other growing industries in the areas where the problems arise. This is of course an extremely hard task, and we do not place as much hope in this policy as we did some years ago.

The third point is that we support the setting up of advisory councils especially to help small- and medium-sized firms with the application of new technologies. We practised this in the case of the watch industry, but too late to rescue a considerable percentage of the jobs.

We also support measures of manpower policy, especially training programmes which prepare workers for other jobs and qualifications. Of course, these were our ideas when we were facing the breakdown of the watch industry. Again we are facing the danger that measures to match the negative effects of technological changes in other industries are being taken too late. There is certainly no way out of these difficulties by stopping technological change. There is even some hope for job preservation by accelerating this change, but we do not want our colleagues to carry the whole burden of these developments. It is to be hoped that we can prove that there is a difference between the eighteenth century and today.

Our bargaining policy is directed to the preservation of the number of jobs on the one hand, and the level of qualification and payment on the other. Some of you may already know that reduction of working hours is one of our high-priority goals.

Concerning the second point, the preservation of the level of qualification and payment, we reached a contract which prevents anybody being transferred to a lower-paid job immediately when technological changes occur. Detailed information on this contract can be given to anybody who is interested.

We shall have to face very serious employment problems in the years to come. Part of these problems, and especially their regional and sector concentration is due to technological change and especially to micro-electronics. The policy measures we are supporting include an advisory system to help in the application of new technology. The workers will have to rely on the strength of their unions and on the results of collective bargaining. We hope that this strength will be increased by the international exchange of ideas and opinions.

## Italian Metalworkers

*Mr Lombardi:* A major step in facing the electronic revolution is dealing with organisation of public demand. Let us take three areas: administration, telecommunications and medical. In administration that means computers, and the control of the market means control of the multinationals. This control is threefold. One way is through legislative action to compel the multinationals to have a balance in producing and selling in the country. In this area we very much need a European union agreement. A second way is through public involvement in development of software products. This point has already been raised. The development of software products such as operating systems, on-line packages and so on, decreases hardware imports by multinationals and this facilitates the development of a secondhand market, which is also a way to limit unjustified innovation.

The third point is the direct struggle of workers to ask for more qualified work. In Italy we asked IBM – and IBM in Italy have 70% of the market with only 58 people occupied in research – we asked IBM to create a laboratory for software research. In telecommunications the present electromechanical switches will last for another 30 years, so there is no hurry to substitute them with electronic switches of multinational companies, especially in those countries such as Italy where 98% of telecommunication demand is public.

On the medical side there is a large possibility of production of new devices arising from electronic technology. The point is to give the people what they really need for their health and not to give them what the medical class needs for their careers. Hence there is a need to strengthen the relationship between unions, physicians and doctors in hospitals.

We are going to organise a conference on these themes in Italy soon. This conference will probably be held in Florence before the end of the year. Much of the industrial automation is in the field of health. Soldering and varnishing is already automised in big industries, but not in the small ones. It is not only by automation that we avoid unhealthy work. We need the direct struggle and interest of the working class to change the work organisation and the causes of bad health: in many plants it is still more profitable to kill a man day-by-day than to replace him with an expensive machine.

Concerning the impact of industrial automation on skills and the relationship between white and blue collar workers. In Olivetti we asked for a wider participation in design phases in tooling shops for some qualified blue collar workers who are working on numerical-control tool machines. In another company, where they make turbines and petrol plants, we asked that the operator of the numerical-controlled tool machine should also be the person who writes the program because at present he only maintains the program. These are traditional blue-collar skills. At the next collective bargaining at the end of the year, we shall ask that such blue-collar skills shall be upgraded to grades to which up to now only white-collar workers have been admitted. These developments are a consequence of electronic innovation.

As a union we are in favour of the development of electronics and all new technologies, but we want the workers to be very much involved in this development. In 1975 FLM first asked that there should be a governmental plan for electronics, containing, first, limits for computer multinationals and telecommunication multinationals; secondly, the development of an Italian-designed electronic switch, which was already under development; thirdly, investments in components; and fourthly, a revision of public administration policy concerning computers. The Italian administration makes extensive use of computers and it is highly inefficient.

At the same time, following FLM's line on workers controlling investment, we have to deal with the main companies on specific aspects within the plan requested by unions. These struggles were hard. At Olivetti there were 60 hours of strikes, at Siemens 98 hours, at IBM 40, at Honeywell 30, and so on. The results were partial but significant. The final government plan contains many bad things, but also some good things that resulted from the workers' struggle.

In spite of the many deficiencies of the government plan, the reactions from the most conservative industries have been ferocious. IBM have pronounced themselves strongly against it, as has STEP, a state group for telecommunications and electronics. This gives you an idea of how planning policy is causing deep conflict within the state industry itself.

Changes in the plan for electronics will be one of the economic battles we shall be fighting. At the same time, FLM will be leading 1½ million metal workers in national bargaining before the end of the year.

## French Metalworkers

*Mr J Lapeyre:* Trade union organisations are discovering the social effects of both computerisation and automation. The impact on employment, both in quantity and in matters of job evaluation, on development of control over the workers, and more generally over citizens, is relevant to individual and public liberties.

The problems connected with data processing are so new and so vast that they demand from the trade union movement a new approach and new solutions. Data processing is not a neutral technology. It builds up our society and hence gives structure to both production and labour.

There are three points at stake revealing the deep connection between data processing and the practice of social domination.

Firstly, computers are produced by a branch controlled by an American monopoly. Actually, at world level, IBM produces 50-60% of the total number of computers in service, which – taking into account the strategic importance of many of these machines – gives it an unbounded power over the economy of the countries concerned. It would only take IBM a few months to cripple these economies by refusing to deliver the spare parts – a policy partially achieved during the Portuguese revolution.

IBM is also a financial power equal to the principal states of the EEC. Facing that disturbing monopoly, some governments have tried to respond by developing strategies like the "plan calcul", a state intervention plan with financial aid granted to the data processing industry, at a national level. Except for ICL which managed to keep a dominant position in Great Britain, and Japan which achieved an ultra-protectionist policy, all other attempts failed. Just remember the failure of the UNIDATA European project, derived from the alliance between Philips from Holland, the CII from France and Siemens from Germany.

A short history of the French data processing industry might be of some interest. CII was born of De Gaulle's government's wish for independence after the refusal of the Americans in 1966 to deliver two computers intended for the French atomic force. It received considerable aid from the state.

From 1967 to 1974, the state's financial aid amounted to 2713 million francs, but the inability of the government to promote the data processing industry at a national level, and jointly at a European level, accelerated the taking over of CII by the American trust Honeywell through its French subsidiary, the Honeywell-Bull company.

This has brought to an end the badly-controlled and badly-led attempts to build a French data processing industry, which could have taken its place at a European level and secured our national independence through the control of this advanced technique.

The FGM-CFDT champions a national data processing industry which should be a real public utility and would allow the various sectors – research, development, production, marketing, services – to be protected, thus allowing the achievement of a complete data processing system.

But let us look at the second challenge set by the data processing industry: data processing is a technique that divides and impoverishes labour while it strengthens and justifies the hierarchical system.

Under its present form, it strengthens the technical division of labour to the profit of those who manage it. It increases the efficiency, the power and the wages of an always small minority of leaders, high salaried staff and experts, whereas at the other end of the scale data processing devalues the skills of masses of workers, including numerous executives whose work loses all its value in matters of autonomy and responsibility. With data processing automation, the clerical employee or the unskilled worker often loses what little interest remained in their job. What was still a "professional gesture" becomes a boring supervisory job, an elementary keying. In matters of preparation of documents or checking of results, the work depends more and more on the machine. Recently, in France, the bank clerks went on strike, demonstrating both the deterioration of the conditions of work linked to automation and the increased division between the mass of clerks and the minority of designers.

In a society that everybody feels to be both complex and fragile, the complexity and simultaneity of decisions leads to the strengthening of the hierarchical powers and to the centralising of information. The hierarchy is changed in character since a large part of the control passes from the now useless foremen to the anonymous machine. Because of the computer, the mere notion of a career is questioned, together with the possibility of acquiring skills in one's job.

The effects due to computerisation and automation have already been noticed in some sectors of high precision mechanics, such as the clock and watch-making or the machine tool industries. The effects are felt at the level of the production through the extreme systemisation linked to the introduction of electronic elements and notably of microprocessing. The effects are felt also at the machine-tool industry level. There is a complete change in the qualification of the professional workers who used to use these machines.

We may anticipate that in the years to come, some sectors as big as the car industry, and the iron and steel industry will also be concerned with the computerisation of the process of production. Then, thousands of jobs will be at stake. Besides the metal industry, one of the crucial problems set by data processing, concerns the rationalising of administrative and management tasks, principally in the tertiary industries – banks, insurance companies and so on. A report has just been published in France, announcing clearly that the sector of office workers would be considerably affected by employment problems. In the banking sector, the installation of new data processing systems will allow for reductions of jobs that could represent, over a period of ten years, almost 30% of the clerical staff – mostly women. The same figures hold true for the insurance companies.

It is quite clear that thanks to cheap investments, investments that will always be cheaper, the savings in productivity would entail some extremely important and negative effects on employment in the sector of tertiary industries.

Since 1968, productivity increases have been greater than production increases in most industries. The main impact of automation will be to widen this gap. The development of the electronic industry and new services will not be enough to replace all the lost jobs in present industries and services. The world economic crisis has only served to speed up demands, but basically the important factor is the huge growth of productivity.

Trade-union claims should be put forward, following that line. As for us, the FGM-CFDT claims a massive reduction of the working week (35 hours), pre-retirement pensions, a five-week holiday, and so on.

Data processing may allow for an increased control by the firms over the activity of the workers and by the state over the private life of the citizens.

The French government had set up a plan to hook up the files that the various ministries hold concerning every citizen individually. That is the SAFARI plan. They would have gathered in the same file, data on his childhood, education, military life, whether he had been up against the law, his case history, information on his political or union activities. The French got upset and did not allow the plan to be carried out, but it is always a temptation for the men-in-power.

Materially, data processing is obviously not neutral and its conception often happens within a structure of social domination. One of IBM's last technological achievements may serve as an example – the electronic switch-board 3750. This system is a real computer with storage and files, allowing all phone calls to be controlled, including the decoding of the phone numbers called to show the list of correspondents outside the firm. On top of that, the 3750, when connected with magnetic badge readers allows control and thus the increase of the rhythm of work, to check productive work, to follow up the movements of the staff. Today, any clerk – or perhaps a shop steward – may be followed step by step within the firm. Some doors may close electronically before him, releasing sound signals while closed circuit television networks record his activities and administration number.

Under the pretence of industrial safety, the system aims at a permanent control over the workers and at dividing them as much as possible. IBM acknowledged it to be true since one of the first ads showing the 3750, ended with a picture of a warder keeping watch on a corridor in a French prison.

Another point of analysis, though still in a prospective field, is the development of communication, say the technology born of the amalgamation of data processing and telecommunications. Here again, IBM has achieved inter-computer connections in real time, and at a high rate, via the German satellite "Symphony". It is thus possible to interconnect files, at an international level, and it also seems that frontiers are abolished and that states will find a substitute in big multinationals such as IBM, which is at present trying to launch its own satellite.

For the FGM-CFDT, laws should be set up to protect the citizens, but it is not enough to secure against the use of data processing. We think that there should be control by the workers from the stage of production. This control should be carried on through public organisations and every citizen ought to have access to the information that concerns him directly.

*Mr Cheyvialle:* Let us take a brief glance at the French EDP industry. Weaknesses clearly appear in the report made by two people at the request of the President of the French Republic. These weaknesses are clearly evident when it forecasts future trends only according to present requirements and sectors. For us it is not adequate to forecast unemployment threats without investigating other development availabilities, for example: production, automation, scientific applications, health care and so on.

Any electronic data processing industry strategy requires a thorough analysis and should be discussed accordingly. The TASS "Policy for the Computer Industry" is a good example of the numerous similarities of our mutual analysis concerning electronics. In it one can read the wish for an alternative strategy, outlined for the creation of an integrated United Kingdom computer industry. If such a policy is not adopted, the industry may soon be a thing of the past.

Computers are, with petroleum and automobiles, one of the largest industries in the world, and the United States companies are still dominating, although no country recommends that the development of an industry of such significance be left to market forces. We are aware that after French loss of control of Bull in 1964, the creation of French CII, which was at the origin of the UNIDATA technology, then the merger of CII and Honeywell-Bull in 1976, 80% of the French market was supplied by American computers. This figure is well above the German, Japanese and British figure, and even above the European average.

We are rather worried about the fact that the US government controls the sales of American-made products and aims to do the same with the sales of German, British and Japanese companies. For us, UFICT-CGT, this is not in the best interests for the French electronic data processing industry workers, executives and so on. UFICT-CGT has made a proposal for the control of this industry by the French: the nationalisation of CII-Honeywell-Bull with legal powers permitting French workers to play a role in the company through what we call democratic management.

There are other situations which are very similar in France and Great Britain, such as integrated circuits policies, the quantity of engineers, executives and technicians in this industry, the necessity for a high-level research and development plan, the possibility of developing strategies other than the multinational companies' one, through ICL in Great Britain and CII-Honeywell-Bull in France. But building a French electronic data processing industry, able to plan its development in compliance with the national interest and to promote technical progress and satisfaction of social needs does not mean protectionism. We are convinced of the possibility of a genuine co-operative relationship, in contrast to one where there is only the brutal and selfish relationship of a multinational company.

That is why, based upon the previously mentioned similarities and principles, and thanks to a great amount of work carried out by UFICT-CGT for its press conference during the SICOB trade fair next week in Paris, we wish to investigate through trade union channels the possibilities of British and French co-operation in the electronic data processing industries. We think that this co-operation could be based upon ICL and CII-Honeywell-Bull. Why is it important that trade unions should establish such relationships? Very briefly, to give strength to worker claims concerning employment, salaries, working conditions, etc, but also to develop proposals concerning the supposedly narrow and unavoidable consequences of unemployment in the near future. We have talked about this previously . . . banks, post office services, secretaries, clerks, etc.

In our view technical progress must help social progress, but this aim can be achieved only if there is a workers' struggle against a low-wage or austerity policy, and for less boring, difficult and dangerous work, massive reduction of hours of work, more qualified work and career possibilities for everybody, better democracy in the companies, and the satisfaction of social needs.

We must prevent any wild industrial restructuring devised solely to maximise the profits of multinational corporations. We must develop a relationship between trade unions that takes into account the multinational strategy – divide to rule.

# 5 Technology and union policy

## Health and Safety

*Ms Vera Meaney:* We in our company have undergone a big changeover in the use of the visual display units, and we are now going to be introduced to the word processors. We have looked into health and safety aspects, taking information from *New Scientist*, the *British Journal of Ophthalmology* and *Computer Weekly*.

We found that emission of microwaves from these machines is implicated in the causation of cataracts. The flicker rate on the machines is also very harmful to people, and it can cause stropocoxic epilepsy. These serious matters are additional to the major health risk to anybody using these machines continuously over a period of time, which is visual fatigue, aggravated by the glare, the reflection and the lack of contrast.

The stresses resulting from a slow computer response time lead to boredom and weariness, and worry from sheer information load. These risks are increased for the users of bifocals and for those people who are on drugs such as valium. Many women are employed in the offices on clerical jobs and a high proportion of women these days are on drugs such as valium. This situation is very harmful to their health.

We have made some recommendations in our company to deal with this, and our company has now turned round and said, "Well, nobody has complained." That is not the answer we want. We want prevention not cure, and the only medical reports that they are taking into account at this time come from the manufacturers. We feel that this is incorrect. They obviously are biased because they are trying to sell us their products. We want an independent report about all the health hazards that are involved with these machines, and we would like to see a fuller report coming out from the union and our Executive Committee on this, to cover ourselves and to be certain that we are not harming our health in any way.

This is a widespread problem and something that people are very worried about. Something further should be done in this field.

*Mr L Clyne:* The union should be dealing with prevention not cure. It is too complacent to say that technology will solve any problems it creates, and that if you introduce technology other jobs will be created elsewhere. The question is: how do we as trade unionists make sure that the problems do not arise in the first place? One of the background documents does refer to the national agreement in Norway, where it has been agreed between the national employers' federation and the Norwegian trade unions that where they are going to plan to introduce the new technology, there should be consultation with trade union membership, right from the first decision. It is important that plans be described in a way which the membership will understand, ie they must be in layman's language.

## Cash Registers

*Mr R Lindsay:* My company makes cash registers. It is not that management does not tell you about things. It is more that they do not know what is going on. One of our divisions makes a cash register – 3000 components in one unit, *x* number of people. Within a year we are going to have a machine out, which is going to be fully electronic, and it is going to have one tenth the number of components. Now we are not mathematicians, but we can see that this will not need the full work force. We have asked management what is going to happen – "What is your intention for these other working people?" The feeling we get is, "Don't worry, it will be OK on the day." And with due respect, this is what we got from Mr Booth this morning. We are not very happy with that point, and we intend, with the help of the TASS Executive, to start recruiting in such a fashion as has not been seen before. We hope to get 100% in the whole Chubb Gross complex.

*Mr J York:* We have gone through the problem that Chubb are going through. We lost 5000 people because we went from electromechanical devices to computers. This was not a Dundee concern. This was done by the management in America. It was a corporate decision. There is nothing that you can do about it, because they will just close down. Are we going to stop producing computers in Dundee and lay another thousand people off? What are we going to do about it? There is literally nothing you can do about it. You have got to try and work out your best strategy – work with them or work against them. If you work against them, they will do what they threatened in Dundee – close the factories down and move on. Dayton in America had 15,000 people in it, working for NCR. It has now got 1500 people working in it. Why? Because in three years they had two strikes of three months duration. That is the way that the multinationals work. NCR now can only employ in any factory up to about 800 people. In Dundee we are lucky. We employ slightly over 1000, because we are a multinational company and we also supply Japan and southern America with certain parts, and we also make more than one type of machine.

But try to fight against the electronic industry on the mechanical side – you just cannot do it, because the shops now are no longer wanting the mechanical machines. Gross took over the NCR product. They are the biggest manufacturer now, and they just took over from NCR. So what are you going to do about it? They will all go the same way as NCR. It is up to your work force to get together and see what can be done. We tried it. The government wanted to give NCR money, but NCR would not accept it. They did not want it. They did not want to have anything to do with mechanical parts. So it is up to you people to find out the best way to do it, because we have tried it and we have failed.

*Mr T Warburton:* It has been said that there is nothing we can do about the advance of this technology. If that is so, we may as well go home now and forget about the situation. In the end the solution is a political solution as to who is going to run these industries, whether they be the industries in this country, whether they be the multinationals or what. We have all said how Albert Booth has skated round the thing. He has because he has concentrated on how we are going to put our little British bit in line with the rest of the world and how we are going to compete with them in this situation.

The presence of our continental friends is a sign of the future. If we are going to defeat this situation, if we are going to bring the thing into line with what we want, then we must do it in the same way as employers do. They have created their multinationals. We will create our multinational unions, and that in the end is going to be the way that we are going to solve it.

**Telecommunications**

*Mr A Marshall:* It has been said on several occasions that the reductions in employment in the industry have come about by the inventions in microelectronics, and that is not altogether true. We are now being caught in that particular trap, but one of the main reasons that we saw reductions within the labour force in 1975, was due to the inept planning by the Post Office in their machinations with Plessey, GEC and STC which is an ITT subsidiary. At that particular time they sought an over-capacity in the old electromechanical systems – and in fact in this country 80% of all telephone calls still go through this system; so it is still there, and then it was heightened by the fact of the demand.

Telecommunications or communications is a barometer of the state of the economy, and if there is world recession then there is no communication, and everything was occupied with that, plus the fact that the financial restraints by the Treasury meant that the Post Office had to tighten its belt anyway. Also some of the proposals of the Post Office showed that it had made tremendous losses. This was questionable accountancy because in subsequent years they have made tremendous profits, fantastic profits.

What we have to stress is that communications is in fact a growth industry. It has always been a growth industry and will continue to be a growth industry, and the figures are from the "Planning of Telecommunications in the UK" by the Department of Applied Economics at Cambridge by Cripps and Godley. In 1976 there were £2000 million spent in Britain on telecommunication services. That is 2% of the gross national product. In fact the three companies which have access to that money are seeking it because it produces fat profits.

It was paralleled at that particular time in the new technology, but it is not now. In fact the managing director of STC in 1972 wrote an article in *Electronics Engineering*, pointing out that there would be, with the advent of the applied technology, substantial reductions within the labour force. So it is not new. There has, in fact been a rapid development in solid-state electronics, not only in systems application, but also in the associated fields which affect employment.

We are gradually being submerged in computer-aided design. At the moment we are only using it in pure tracing methods by using Calma operations. It is feasible, and the design parameters have been turned out, so that in fact a circuit engineer can feed in the appropriate data which would turn out all the documents, all the drawings, all the wiring information, all the NC information, from particular information fed in, thereby cutting out several job functions normally carried out by people in that industry. At the same time it has been applied in manufacturing. We are getting more and more automated processing, so that there will be little or next to no assembly. It is affecting the maintenance areas insofar as it is self-monitoring and self-curing, and therefore the maintenance repair will be greatly reduced.

Recession enables the Post Office and the private companies to change over from this very highly intensive industry to a huge profit-making, labourless business. The quoted figures are that if we were to maintain with digital telephone exchanges, which is the latest technology, and we obtained 20% of the export market world, it is estimated that 70,000 jobs would go within the industry. That is a lot of jobs within this particular industry.

The development at the moment of our business hangs on the so-called System X, which needs to be exportable if the industry is to survive. This seems unlikely because it is not compatible with international requirements.

Christopher Layton, a director in the Electronics, Telecommunications and Computers Directorate General of the EEC, has said that they have looked at the infrastructural problems that confront the EEC. They are aware of the immense power of the multinationals and countries like Japan which operate a state, bank and industry role. They are looking at a long term programme. They are not just looking at a system, X25 Euronet, which will cope with the normal means of making a telephone call, but they are also looking at data transmission, the data bank for scientific purposes, and central and all other facets of communication (for example, delivering mail by electronic mail instead of having a postman).

They are seeking a communications service which will be standardised to the EEC. They have seemingly made a political decision, and they say that ITT is non-European, which is a bit of an odd statement, because they seem to control a substantial amount of the telephone business in Belgium and Spain. What he is saying that the capability of the UK industry needs to be strengthened, and indeed at the moment, they seem to be putting the eggs in the basket of Philips, Siemens and L M Ericsson, which is Swedish and not part of the EEC. They are therefore seeking joint developments, and they reckon that there is a need for public and social accountability.

The point to be stressed is that they are trying to set up a standardised situation, and if we do not get political pressures to either identify that problem, or to ensure that System X is of a design which can be sold internationally, then that reflects on the capability of our industry to survive, and that means that we may lose more jobs.

In the international field, Plesseys found themselves in their latest venture, to be partners with Western Electric; that is, the largest American company in the telecommunications business. In a bid for the Saudi Arabian contract, a complete government contract, we lost out. And the irony of the contract is that not only when you are bidding in that sort of way do you have to be experienced inside your sort of field of expertise, that is telecoms, but you have also got to take on, in our particular case, all the civil engineering facilities that would be required to put in a tele-communications business – buildings, telegraph poles, transmission aerials, all the associated peripheral parts that go with it. There is a certain amount of apprehension that what could be a lucrative billion dollar profit-making contract, could also be a billion-dollar-losing contract. We cannot talk for the economies of a lot of the governments which are now seeking a position. In fact Plesseys have got a contract with a small part of South Africa, called Transkei. Visibly, it is bankrupt, and is purely dependent on South Africa for its economy anyway, but the fact is that we are selling telecommunication equipment there, with no real guarantee that we shall get the cash for it.

We shall be in competition internationally with America, Japan or the EEC. The future is looking rather bleak

Then coupling the telecommunications industry with other major developments in microelectronics and computers, we have to break the economic structures which we are operating in. If we do not get to the political position of trying to break these constantly restraining economic factors, then we will be restrained within a close-thinking philosophy. We will apply the same capitalist economics in seeking the solutions, and the solutions from that will not be the right ones.

We should be seeking to invest inside manufacture. We are not getting guarantees that the revenue from North Sea oil will be invested in any of our industries in a way that will give accountability to the workers in this country. We are not achieving that political objective, and we have to ensure that we can build that sort of objective. We have to attain that, so that we can start giving written guarantees for the future, for our children. We are living on borrowed time, on revenue available from North Sea oil.

## Petrochemicals

*Mr I Parr:* ICI has a policy, publicly stated, that it intends to reduce its staff by 2½% per annum. What happens when they get down to two or three people I do not know.

There are advantages and disadvantages in computer usage. Computers in process control cause problems because of too few skilled staff, a problem partly created by ICI themselves. There is a shortage of skilled instrument artificers who are needed to keep the transmitters going and the parts of the plant that send signals to the computers. Computer control allows the design of safer plant. Also benefits can be derived from the use of scarce raw materials.

The second computer level is databases. These are really a sort of glorified library stacked with the necessary information. In ICI there are links with other databases all over the world. So it is possible, given a particular subject, to follow it up through the various reference works, to use key-words to derive information on any particular subject. We can use them for getting information for the union. I have got a very thick book there which gives a list of all the published data on health and safety in the UK. The problem that the company has is in what they call technology transfer. Their problem is simply that they do not know who needs what information and why they need it. This is an area which should concern us a lot, because, whilst we have access to the information at the moment, it may be that we shall not have that sort of freedom in the future.

The third area, already mentioned, is word processors. Our experience is that it has reduced the number of girls in one office – I am afraid that they are all girls – by a factor of five or six, and a couple of them are redundant. The growing number of technical reports are fed into the database.

The fourth area is computer-aided design. We design using computers. We use them for calculations. We register equipment so that we can call things up, and we also have material listing. So we operate a total range of computer possibilities. At the moment, the one thing that the computer cannot do is the conceptual work in chemical plant design. As in most engineering, that is extremely difficult for the company to initiate.

There are two particular problems. One is the fact that generally we have engineers who are trying to initiate these systems. There is obviously a problem of skills, the problem of people having the right skills for the job. The other problem is that the engineers who are trying to define the job are not the draughtsmen who do it, so while we have got that situation occurring we are in a fairly safe position because the company has not yet thought of borrowing the skills of the draughtsman and trying to put them into the computer. In fact our members are making pretty sure that it does not develop that way.

The advantage is that we do design much better using computers. We are putting expertise into particular areas of design that we had never bothered to go into before, and these have created a whole new range of jobs. Nowadays we do not use the rule-of-thumb method. We design the thing properly, and this again makes for better and safer plants.

There has been a 2½% reduction of staff in ICI in the last two years or 18 months or so. It has been running at the rate of about 4000 people a year, so it is a bit more than 2½%, except in the department where I work. The reason for this is partly because of computer-aided design, because it restricts the amount of work that can be sent out to be done by outside organisations. More important, you cannot use computers unless you have got a commitment to capital investment, and currently the investment programme in Mond Division where I work, is way above what it was a few years ago. It is way above the average for the company. The result is that we are not reducing the staff in our department. We are actually increasing the numbers. The union has said, on a number of occasions, how important investment is. We are talking about the microelectronic industry and the sort of changes that are going to be made in labour patterns. We have to link this policy about the way in which we organise work, with a policy of insisting that the money that is created in fact goes back into further investment in plant.

## Word Processing

*Miss C Bloomfield:* The health hazards of VDUs, already discussed, probably also apply to word processors.

Word processors are used in government, with a lot of standard work to put out, but in, for example, customer accounting and customer correspondence, a junior could do the job. Word processors in this area would take away the creative aspect of correspondence work. It would also mean getting rid of most typist and secretarial jobs.

There has been talk of multinational unions. Soon there will not be so many jobs left with people to be in unions, so had we not better hurry up if we are to catch up with the job loss?

## Social Implications

*Mr P Ward:* Reference has been made to the people who leave this country and go to the States for the money and so on. Of course this is not a problem that is only applicable to this country. In fact the problem is far worse in some of the third world countries where a great deal of the resources are being used in educating people. These people are gradually being enticed away from the country that has spent all the money on their education, to the affluent nations. So we are in great danger of finishing up with countries like America, or perhaps even states within America, having people with academic and intellectual qualifications far superior to those in the rest of the world. This is a great tragedy and a totally wrong direction for people if we are concerned about the future of mankind.

So this is something that international trade unions, and anyone who is concerned with the future of international relationships and welfare should be looking at more seriously, because if that development continues, obviously the third-world countries are never going to be in a position where they can develop and produce their own wealth and their own decent society.

What we are going to see is that it is going to be more and more the multinationals that are controlling. By their very flexibility, and the opportunities that these new developments offer them, they are going to find their havens with dictatorships, with the small island communities, the tax havens and so on, where they will surround themselves and become more or less invulnerable to the kind of international trade unionism that we are looking for.

When people talk about us keeping ahead of technology, what do they mean? Are we going to produce with one man the whole of the world's supply of motor cycles in somewhere like Taiwan? Are we going to produce the whole of the world's shipbuilding in somewhere like Korea? We cannot all produce more and more and more. We cannot all be more efficient and more effective.

Albert Booth talked about the IMF putting pressure on this country, and cutting our social spending and so forth, causing a loss of jobs. If you recall, that loan was £3.4 billion. Not only did we cut public expenditure,

and cut the wages of our people who could have created more employment
in both those spheres, but we also sold a vital part of our North Sea oil,
our future insurance against exploitation and so on.

That loan was £3.4 billion; now during that period, the government
raised in government securities £7.8 billion – over twice as much in
three months. So therefore there was plenty of private capital in this
country to cover the government expenditure without borrowing from
abroad. What they failed to realise, of course, was that during that time
we had all agreed in the trade unions to have a 5% wage ceiling, and yet
the government at the same time that it had got the workers to accept this,
was inducing the capitalists and the wealthy in this country to invest in
government stocks, by offering 14% return. So we got 5% return for the
worker and 14% for those who had private capital to invest. And the cost
of borrowing that private capital worked out at a cost to us of £3 million
a day for the next 20 years.

So those are the kind of things that we are talking about. We are talking
here about wage differentials. We will finish up with very high pay for a
very small and specialised group of people. We will continue to have the
kinds of divisions of class which have caused so much controversy and so
many of the problems that we have had in this nation.

People are making these new devices and new processes, and in many
of these very specialised areas, people get intellectual blinkers. They are
only interested in their own particular sphere, and they cannot look at the
social consequences of what they are producing. At one time when the
bosses and the staff workers in, say, the mills and the textile industries,
brought in new techniques they could see the starvation and deprivation
that they were causing. This caused some of them to feel the repurcussions
of those consequences. Now you are going to have a situation where you
are going to have these people living in somewhere like California, and
the repercussions taking place in somewhere like Amsterdam or Rochdale
or wherever it might be, throughout the rest of the world. I think that we
should make it clear through the trade union movement, and try, by
encouraging these people to join the trade union movement, to realise
that they will be responsible for the kind of society that they develop.

None of us has really touched on the whole basis and concept of trade.
Is it producing more and more and ramming it out across your shores for
people who do not really want it or cannot really afford it or whatever?
Or has the whole really basic trade been bastardised by the multinationals?
Trade is for people who want to sell us what we want to buy. So really I
think that we should start looking at the whole concept. We should say:
what is trade for? And is it not time that we really looked at the whole
concept of trade, and looked at what some of the more progressive under-
developed countries are now saying, when they say that they want to
produce their own motor cars and telecommunications, we cannot say

"No, for God's sake don't do that because it will mean that we shall have tremendous unemployment in this country." We should see that this is a reasonable demand that these people are making, and we should organise ourselves in this country well in advance.

Our colleagues in the press have a key role to play. As long as they tell us that we need to produce more and more, as long as they tell us that the fashion demands this, that two companies must produce a million and a half cars a year to be viable, and that we must all have the same kind of car with the same kind of equipment – as long as they dictate those kind of terms then we will start to believe that that is what we must have. If they dictate to us that we want and need tax cuts, then we will all demand more tax cuts, and there will be even more cuts in public expenditure.

This all comes down to what kind of social structure, what kind of social planning we are going to see. I see that we need some kind of export control situation. We as the highest consumer market in the world are in a superb situation to demand that. What perhaps the media should be saying is: look for job satisfaction; look for things that are custom-built that you want to see; look for craft orientation and so on.

Did we not learn by the high-rise flats and the bureaucracy in Swansea with the taxation departments and so on – have we not learned the lesson? Would it not be ideal for this kind of technology, instead of having a massive headquarters in Houston or wherever it might be, for use to have them in the homes and in the local post office, where they are providing a real service to us all? Instead of one massive computer centre, we would have thousands of smaller centres all round the country, doing all kinds of things in the home. That would create far more jobs than this centralisation has brought about. Also this centralisation puts the control in central hands. We have got to decide who controls and who decides? The trade unions and the people, or the establishment and capitalism?

Industrial democracy is going to be looking beyond a two or three years horizon. We are going to be saying that we want to look at the future beyond these two or three years, and making sure that we shall not wait as we always have in the past. If we do not find social and political answers to this question, there is going to be a far graver danger, because people who are unemployed and people who are frustrated are going to backlash against society. There is a grave danger that that back-lash will result in fascism.

## Sex Discrimination

*Miss C Wootton:* It is important to appreciate that computer-aided manufacture is already with us. Perhaps the shop floor is only now beginning to wake up to the implications of the new devices for their jobs.

The implications for staff are also quite serious, because if the company is going to invest vast amounts of money in computer-aided manufacture, they are going to want to get the return on that investment. The way to do that is to work shift systems. Now if the work force on the shop floor are required to work shift systems, then there is obviously a requirement for staff workers to work shift systems. The implications of this for women are very grave; because of the lack of social facilities for women in the way of nursery care and day care it is virtually impossible for most women to work shift systems. Therefore the employers are now going to be saying: "We are not going to train you for this job because you won't work the shifts that go with this job." So yet again, women are going to be deprived of the ability to enter the more qualified jobs.

Another item is computer bureaux. At the moment I operate an electro-mechanical accounting machine, which the company are trying to replace by an American Texas Instruments 770 intelligent terminal. Now Texas Instruments have done a survey. They have had a look at the systems program, and they have decided what we want in our program, what the program will do and what information we will get, and when we will get it.

Now we have been to the company and we have said to them, "What are the implications on the work force? What are the operating times? How many operators are going to be required to use it? Who is going to analyse the information that comes off the computer? What facilities have you made available for education and the retraining of the people employed? And they have sat back and said, "We don't know yet." And that is not good enough. So we have said to them, "Until you put it in writing and you give us firm guarantees that the only people working that equipment when it is introduced will be the people at present employed at the plant, that they are going to receive the correct remuneration for operating the equipment, and that there will be no job loss, then you are not having that machine on site. We are not going to use it."

In a lot of plants these sort of visual display units and systems have already been installed. They are just creeping in.

We have got to recruit the people who work in these computer bureaux, because a lot of the stuff is done outside your plant. You have no control over what goes into the program and because you do not understand the program and you do not see the program, you do not know how much of what you do is being monitored by that machine. You do not know whether it is monitoring, as we saw on that film "The Chips are Down", how many mistakes you make, how many characters you depress a minute, and what sort of a record is being kept about your performance. We really have got to go out and recruit the people who work in these computer bureaux – the software merchants. Until we control it from there, we have got no chance.

**Aerospace**

*Mr J Burgess:* I started life as a loftsman dealing with surface geometry. In the days of early NC, we interrogated surfaces, produced hand-drawn profiles and filled in these drawn profiles to design office engineering drawings. Subsequently, with the aid of a rule and glass we lifted off dimensional data which enabled NC engineers to produce tapes and a finished component. This is obviously extremely time-consuming. It was inaccurate, and the outcome was that the program accepted data, the basic profiles of which were not controlled, so the next step from that was to produce a program which set up a computer data bank, controlling surfaces. Having done this, we move along in time to producing information which would be translated into data acceptable by machines which are capable of producing graphical output.

We had one of these machines installed. Not only were we then able to produce a drawing at a particular scale, but also numerical control data to an accuracy of four places of decimals, which was used by NC engineers.

The next step was the advent of VDUs in 1971. This ensured immediate access to data banks to produce tapes to supply information to a draughting machine to produce graphical output. Then we move to the advent of Tectronix equipment, which will produce on a screen a graphical representation of what you may have hidden somewhere in the computer.

Ultimately, during this period of time, the aerospace industry had changed from De Havillands to Hawker Siddeley. We became involved in projects between various sites, who do not hold the same type of information on the same type of computer, using the same type of programs.

We found that within the area in which we were working, we required to produce our own programs, so we then produced our own particular program software in-house. This meant that we had control of the data that we put into the programs, the structure of the programs, the maintenance, and all the other facets of computer-based programs.

With the nationalisation of the aircraft industry, we now found that we had become involved in what was BAC. BAC had gone along different lines to Hawker Siddeley, and we found difficulty in the early days of transfer of data between Hawker Siddeley sites. We now have the same problem of transfer of data between the ex-BAC and the Hawker Siddeley sites under the guise of British Aerospace.

The problem is that during the course of numerous redundancies and early retirements, we find that the labour force that we were able to train and bring into a field of which previously they had no knowledge, is not available. Whilst we have a considerable amount of work which necessitates, even with computer usage, a fairly large work force, the people and the training just do not seem to be available.

## Computer-Aided Design

*Mr J Holton:* The problems will only be resolved if we can get some measure of co-operation with our colleagues in other countries. But that is not to say that there is nothing that we can do in our individual companies.

The problem should be attacked on two levels. Obviously we cannot cope with multinational companies with a national union, and we have got to get more co-operation with other unions abroad. But we can still do something within our own companies. It is not practical to resist on a general basis the introduction of computer technology, but that does not mean to say that we have to accept any application. It does not mean to say that we should not have a voice in what kind of computer technology we get. The key here is that we must be strong, and that we must recruit every possible member, so that we are in a position when the company wants to introduce computer technology, to say, "Well, convince us then, because it is not coming here until we are convinced." And then we have got to say, "Well, if you are going to introduce this computer technology only our members may operate it. We are not having non-members on this. We are not allowing any non-members to accumulate expertise in its operation."

Two years ago in our company they brought in computer-assisted draughting. This equipment has been built up and there are now five input units. There is no doubt that this is the shape of things to come. There are still a lot of draughtsmen who think that their job cannot be computerised. Well, make no mistake about it – it can. I would be very surprised if in 10 years we are still using pencils in drawing offices.

We had to be convinced by the company that it was necessary to keep abreast of these computer applications and secondly they had to agree to the terms on which it should come in. Firstly, it would only be brought in to a limited extent and then there would be a two year period after which we would discuss it again. Secondly, no non-members would be allowed to operate the equipment or be involved with it in any way. After a great deal of trouble this was achieved.

The main problem now is to develop effective policies for controlling computer applications and to educate members so that when these things happen to them, they know what is happening and are able to cope with it. In most companies if they want to bring in a computer technology, members just do not know how to tackle the situation. They do not know how to handle it.

We must develop the policies and we must get them over to the members. We must recruit every possible member so that we are strong enough to resist it. Most of us at this conference are not going to be involved in any international applications. At the grass roots we have got to deal with it where it first comes. It is very important that we should not have a sense that it is hopeless and that it is either a political problem or an international problem. It is our problem just as well and we have got to learn to cope with it.

*Mr J Turner:* It has been suggested that CAD was introduced into design areas to make up for particular skill shortages. That is not true. Design aids have been introduced to supplement the draughtsman's skill. Now, because of the increased need for accuracy in the design of microcircuits, the draughtsman is no longer capable of working to that degree of accuracy, and so requires some sort of aid.

Within ICL the aids have been introduced without the people who have actually been working with these things being aware of the implications for their job.

When we have to have these aids introduced into a drawing office or wherever, we must be totally involved with the implications of that bit of equipment. We must be aware of what it does, and what it is going to do to us and to the future generations.

We have got to insist that where traditional skills are being phased out, with the help of these computer aids, that industry must be forced to put something back in to replace the traditional skill. They have got to be made to reorganise, retrain, to send back to school to learn a new and hopefully useful job in society, and at the end to make up for all the disappointments that apparently this computer technology will bring to individual careers.

*Mr J R Painter:* British Aerospace has a rather large investment in CAD. We use it in stress, aerodynamics, lofting programmes, computer-aided machining and a number of design management systems as well. We get a lot of benefits from CAD. The obvious ones are that we get better designs, designs that are far more accurately optimised, more precise. We can do far more checks on the aircraft. Some of the designs that we do now probably could not have been designed without a computer. The Airbus wing that we undertook is a very advanced critical wing, and we would probably never have achieved the design of a wing like that without a computer.

We have had our redundancies. Most of them have probably been the responsibility of the recession as much as various political decisions which have affected and devastated our industry, rather than the introduction of any CAD techniques. We are now on the verge of introducing draughting systems using mini-based computers, which now give us the chance to have a large number of computers scattered around sites – a comparatively large number anyway – for the same price as a mainframe of a few years ago. The development of microprocessors is going to advance us even further through that stage.

One of the reasons that we look at computer draughting systems is that now that we are expanding, we have more projects to do, and we cannot get the staff of the calibre we need, having made them all redundant. But the main reason that we are introducing them is the fact that in order to compete effectively with the world's aerospace industries, we have to have very much more advanced techniques in designing aeroplanes. The Americans are already quite a long way ahead of us in the field of computer-aided draughting. There are a number of advantages. We can improve the quality of the product very much. We remove a lot of the mundane parts of the job of draughting, allowing the designer to spend more time concentrating on detailed aspects of design, which a lot of the designers would consider to be the more interesting parts of design. We are also aware of the fact that we have to take account of the fact that there are people who in fact enjoy some of the more ordinary parts of draughting. Drawing is an art to a certain extent, particularly the high accuracy drawing that is carried out in the lofting, and there are people who enjoy doing that. We will have to accept that computer-aided systems must take into account that there are people who still want to carry on in their traditional roles.

It is very much harder to try to stop developments head on that to deflect them in the direction that we want them to go.

*Mr P Gage:* Sooner or later, if your firm says that they want to introduce computer technology in the form of CAD, CAM or something like that, you have got to get down to finding out what your members are going to get out of it. The union is tending to let us down. We are talking about data banks, computer connections and things like that, but at Baker Perkins we had the introduction of CAD and it went through all the regular channels. It took us about a year to accept it, but then when we turned to the union saying: "Look, we have got this particular situation. Can you give us any other relevant data as to other firms within the district or within the country with whom we can compare our situation?" And the answer was a complete blank.

Neither on financial grounds nor health and safety grounds could we get any answer at all. We got a fairly good deal in the end. Perhaps we digressed a little with details, but we managed to get the position that after 148 hours of training on CAD, you got £100 consolidated into your salary, and after another period of time, depending on the utilisation that you get, and this is on a progressive scale, you could get over and above that £100, for another 425 hours, which is roughly six months, you could get another £200 consolidated on to your salary. So you then get a total of £300 extra for using CAD.

We then had another situation where they wanted to introduce CAPRFI (Computer Aided Planning and Rate Fixing), and thought of a different approach. We took the same context of the CAD agreement and we got this on a group basis. So we now have a much better situation where we have a group of 40 people who, whether they are trained on it or not at this particular stage, get an increment of £75 per annum, another one coming up of £25 equal to the £100 training period, by this December, and then the utilisation payments after that are as and when we use it.

We are talking about these firms having data banks. Why can the union not have a data bank, so that when you are faced with a situation similar to this, you can refer to some specific point in the union, and say, "We have this situation about to arise in our factory, what other advice can you give us? What other relevant firms are there within this district and within this country as a whole, with whom you can compare your situation and say, 'This is what we want to aim for.'?"

## National Enterprise Board

*Mr Bob Hardie:* Within the Scottish Division of Ferranti, the five-year plan which is required from them by the National Enterprise Board indicates a growth of 28% in staffing requirements, which will be evenly distributed between manual and staff employees. In parallel with this welcome envisaged growth, there is the expansion of computer-aided design and manufacturing, the introduction of automated test equipment – all part of the plan, and coming up outside the plan, word-processing. And why is this being done? The rate of introduction of such new increased capital investment is overtly acknowledged within the plan as being influenced by a shortage of technically qualified staff.

If you look a bit closer at the figures, covertly the plan is acknowledged as contributing to increased profitability. The result however is that there will be fewer jobs than there otherwise would have been in an expanding sector.

Job gain within Ferranti is job loss in Plessey, in Mullard, and in all the suppliers of discrete components, and job loss among sub-contractors that made the packages for a previous bulkier generation of products. A job can be done at domestic level and has to be done. It has to be tackled as the day to day problems come up at office committee level. There is a need for involvement of the wider trade union movement, an overall planned response. The TASS "Policy for the Computer Industry" talks about enlarging the NEB stake in Ferranti and other firms. As part of the policy, it would seem to me not to miss the mark but to fall short of it. Why? Because as long as NEB works on commercial and market criteria, as long as labour remains a commodity treated as other commodities, whether the ownership be nominally private or public, then we are long way from the aim of controlling industry in the interests of the community. Albert Booth has said that we have now forged political and industrial organisations to meet the challenge. I am saying that none of these organisations has yet fitted itself for the change in pace that we are now facing.

## Shipbuilding

*Mr A Cowey:* Swan Hunter have only nine people employed in the computer department. The company over the years has strategically placed them in ivory towers, so the members over the years have always considered them to be a separate body of people.

There have been efforts "to get 19½-year-old clever boys, who are doing well at night school, to come into the computer department and learn what is going on," but the company refused to do this. However, we may have to do a lot more computer work than we do now to get orders against the rest of the world.

Two men in British Shipbuilders, Newcastle, claimed that efforts were being made to look into "all the computer requirements in Britain" for the company. Swan Hunters have IBM, Cammell Lairds have ICL, and so on, but there was no clear picture of what the industry would be like in five years.

We cannot be optimistic ("Eric shut Rolls Royce this morning, Alan has just finished 20,000 off at Plessey"). Grass roots members may decide what sort of computer work comes into the office and how much it is going to cost the company, but there is little to warrant enthusiasm about computers.

## Alternative Technology

*Mr J D Shutt:* There is an assumption contained in a lot of the contributions that should be examined. The assumption is made that if an enterprise decides to change its product range to include the new technology, then that is the only application of the skills and expertise of the people working in that plant that can be considered.

We are failing or avoiding considering the fundamental question of examining what it is that we produce, why we produce it, how we produce it and for whom. It is a basic contradiction to say that just because someone somewhere cannot make a profit that that group of workers is redundant. They are only redundant to that particular employer's set of needs. They are not redundant, in my opinion, to our needs, and they are certainly not redundant to society's needs, and that is why the union has got to start looking at alternative production and alternative forms of control. It is not the introduction of technology so much that is the problem, it is the use to which it is put which is the problem.

Albert Booth talked about not believing that there were any necessary links between technological change and unemployment. He mentioned the welding and paint-spraying application of robotic equipment in the motor industry. And it is true that it has beneficial effects. It has eliminated the tedious, monotonous, dirty aspects of production work. Its relative acceptance has been because it has done that, also because those people displaced in the process have been absorbed. This is relatively few people in the context of the complete plan. But it has not yet begun to touch other functions which do not have the same beneficial spin-off.

Every crisis that we go through means that we appear to face the problem that we have a decimation of our manufacturing capability, and a decimation and elimination of skills. I believe that the argument should be portrayed that instead of elimination of skills we should be talking about the positive utilisation of them. If that means diversification, then it should be on socially-useful products.

There is a massive range of commodities that society needs and that society will support, but which will not be produced merely because either they are not considered profitable or because someone somewhere believes that their production would effect the profitability of something else. It is that mentality, and that political viewpoint that has got to be challenged.

The only guarantee against technological change destroying jobs and working conditions has got to be at the grass roots with alert membership, that understands what a company is trying to replace, understands that the on-the-job action in a united and disciplined fashion is the only safeguard that we have got at this time. Technical knowledge without activity will get us nowhere, just as activity without knowledge is like fighting with your arms behind your back.

Head office should continue to publish special literature dealing with the problem. TASS News should produce regular publications with special articles on the subject, and this conference should be expanded into the divisions with seminars and weekend schools. The Research Department should attempt to compile a TASS procedural clause which can be applicable to dealing with technological change and the issues which we face.

If our membership has the knowledge and the understanding, it will be better prepared to defend itself. Knowledge is the prerequisite in fighting against the harmful effect of this technological change. Essentially we have got to take away the mystery that is built up within this field, and which the companies find very useful to exploit.

As plants become more complicated, that in turn increases our industrial power. We shall get more control over production if we use our heads, educate ourselves as to the problems, and question in whose interests technology is being applied.

## Computer Staff Organisation

*Mr R Cooper:* Everybody is agreed that what is needed is grass-roots activity to tackle this problem. We have got some measure of international co-operation. We have got a federation in Europe of engineering unions. We have had some successes. Italian workers have blocked a 35 million Italian government investment in Honeywell, because it did not suit their criteria. In this country the government is following union policy in that it has set up the National Enterprise Board, which has got stakes in the very companies that we want to recruit in – that is, computer manufacturing companies like Ferranti, software houses like CAP, Logica, System Designers. But obviously the main work that we have got to do is at the grass roots.

At my own site CAD is done in two companies. One has long had a well-organised drawing office, and when CAD was introduced, existing draughtsmen were trained in the new technology.

The other company had a problem in that they had a massive requirement for very complicated printed circuit boards, and they responded to that problem by introducing their own equipment and recruiting their own staff. They were ex-hairdressers, part-time students, people who could be brought in afresh and be paid less, and trained only for the new technology. These people are, by and large, non-members. So we saw a change in the way that the company was operating its computer-aided design facility.

It meant that the bulk of the work is done in a non-union area. To make the company accountable for investment for training, we have first to recruit members. Employers will try and choose areas where union membership is weakest and implement the new technology there.

It has been said that we should recruit the bureau staff, because these are the people who are producing the products which are affecting designers and engineers. Well, we are doing that. We have set up, under the aegis of the National Computer Industry Advisory Panel, regional committees. We have one functioning in London and our objective is to act as an information-exchanging forum, so that people who have no idea what the rate for a particular job is, can find out. We can actually service the members where the job is too complex for head office.

Software house staff are just as exploited and manipulated as those who have to use their products, and that is one of the reasons why we are concentrating on that area. If you really feel that you need the information and that you are not informed enough, then you really cannot just expect to get on the end of a telephone and get that information. The best thing is to communicate to each other, because the knowledge is in the union. All that is required is for that information to flow from our members to the members who need the information.

# 6    Closing remarks

*Mr J Tuchfeld:* Firstly, TASS supports technical innovation, it always has done. After all, a great many TASS members spend their working lives eliminating the jobs of manual workers. We can hardly change our line because now we are affected, but it is a sign of the change in our society that for the first time white-collar workers are affected by changes of this kind.

We also have to admit that in many respects the computer technology being introduced does the job better than human beings. It is a sign of the shame of our society that, instead of welcoming that, we are in a state of gloom and despondency. But although white-collar workers are affected, the first group to be affected have, as always, been the manual workers. In the telecommunications industry, thousands of manual workers have been sacked by the change to System X. In the TV industry, 10 years ago a TV set had 1500 parts. It now has 600. In Japan it is 400. In two years time it will be 400 here.

The major impact has been on women workers and part-time workers. We have seen the end of the twilight shift, the elimination of electro-mechanical assembly. And just as women workers have been hardest hit in manual employment, if we are not careful they will be the hardest hit in white-collar employment as well, because employers will resist training part-time workers for the new more highly-skilled jobs that the computer society demands.

The immediate impact upon TASS has been in drawing offices. We have seen the virtual elimination of printed-circuit draughtsmen. We are seeing the elimination of body draughtsmen, of electrical draughtsmen. In a few years time a whole range of detail work will no longer be performed on a board. But this is within the framework of a total increase of technical employment, and we have to fight in each firm to be sure that the jobs which are developing in our industry are available to those who are otherwise being displaced.

Yet the employers' record is not very good. In 1967, the engineering industry had 311,000 trainees. In 1974, it had 191,000 and the greatest percentage reduction was in craftsmen and technicians, the group that the employers are now crying from the housetops for, wondering why it happened. They should know. They caused it. Similarly in the clerical and administrative field, the introduction of computers will provide a massive amount of information which was previously unobtainable. That information has to be handled by human beings. It will generate new employment. It is essential that those who are displaced, and who include a significant number of part-time women workers, should be able to perform these functions.

Another point concerns the potential conflict between manual and white-collar workers, with prototype work by-passing the drawing office and with maintenance work either being done remotely by miniature TV cameras, or by technologists rather than by time-served men. It is absolutely essential that TASS takes the lead to ensure that worker does not fight worker. We of all unions are the most easily able to give such a lead, because we are part of a union which includes every worker in engineering.

Yesterday the unions reached agreement in Ford for the introduction of computers. It was an 8-point programme and included no redundancy. Productivity improvements would lead to salary increases for all. The status quo clause would apply for any attempt to introduce shift work or any change in head count. Skills would be rewarded. There would be an adequate training programme. The TUC's Chief Medical Officers would be invited to contact the company's Chief Medical Officer to discuss the health implications of the use of visual display units. All information acquired specifically or incidentally by computer-based systems should not be used for individual or collective work performance assessment. However that is not much more than establishing a Geneva convention for the work that will now take place in the plants when computers are actually put into use. But it is a sign that we do understand the need to have a policy and deal with it.

We are going to produce a wide range of information. There is a document in front of the Executive giving guidelines on how we can keep our members informed, and the best way to deal with these issues.

It is one thing dealing with your own firm. You cannot in your own firm deal with national policy. Employment has declined in engineering by half a million in the last 10 years. There are now fewer employed in engineering than there were 20 years ago, and this tendency to decline will continue. Technological change is taking place at such a rapid rate that a massive increase in production can now be provided without any increase in the number of people employed. We have heard politicians say that the way that that is resolved is by increasing the service industries. Yet when it comes to health and education, which are the major service industries, we have both government and opposition vying with each other to assure everyone that they are not going to increase taxation to increase public expenditure. It is the height of political cynicism to say on the one hand that the services shall be increased, and then tell the people that their taxes will not go up as a result.

We also have to campaign at national level for a shorter working life – start work later, finish work earlier, have a shorter working year, but that is not something that can be easily dealt with in individual firms. And we have to ask how this can be achieved. We have lessons to learn. The first industrial revolution brutalised a generation. It led to starvation, deportation, both voluntary and forced, and those who in frustration tragically rebelled, were shot or hanged. But now we are in a different situation. The employers are the same, but we are not. We now have a strong organised trade union movement, and we have to win the trade union movement for a line that will succeed.

First of all, shift work. It is obvious to us that the obsessive desire of the society in which we live, that makes profit the sole criterion, will demand the increase of shift work. We will soon be told the modern equivalent of Lord Newcastle in the House of Lords, who explained that children should work in the pits because it improved family life, because children of five could be working with their fathers. I am sure that we shall soon be told that shift work improves family life.

Similarly, the employers nationally and internationally have got together to resist a shorter working year. It is quite clear that there is an international campaign by the employer to ensure that the benefits of the new technology shall not accrue to us.

Already those like myself involved in multinational company negotiations, find that on the one hand we are told in France they do not have a 40-hour week, so how could we ask for less, or if you are talking about white collar workers, "How dare you ask for less than 37½ because no-one else in Europe has got less than 40?" But I would remind you that the Belgian workers fought successfully for a reduction to the shorter working week this year, and we should all throughout Europe applaud their action.

The employers work on the principle of divide and rule. They always have. And they are always concerned about key areas. It is no accident that the British Raj believed that railways were the most important thing in India, so they made sure that they had a pliant Anglo-Indian community to run them.

Similarly in industry until a few years ago the white-collar workers were a corrupt labour force. They were the team of blacklegs in industry, but now that has ended. White-collar workers are now substantially unionised. But now there is a new group of key workers in our society, those who work in computers, and it is absolutely essential that they are organised. If they are not organised they will be like the Anglo-Indian community in India.

They will be the group who can be relied upon by the employers to ensure that industry still ticks over whatever the workers do.

So it is important for everybody that the computer workers are organised, not least for their benefit, but because in the end the non-unionisation of white-collar workers in Britain did not help them. In the end, if it suited the employers, they got the sack like everybody else.

We believe that this new technology can provide benefits for all mankind. But that can only be achieved if we make it like that, and we face an ideological battle. We also face a consistent campaign that suggests that those who are unemployed should be ashamed, that workers should be encouraged to sell their jobs for a lump sum, that those who want supplementary benefit are scroungers, that nothing counts provided that you yourself are at work. That is the ultimate in divide and rule. We have to win the ideological battle to say that the technological change must lead to a better life for all. We have to say that if our society cannot provide that, then we have to change that society.


*Chairman:* The problem is not that a new technology is being introduced but that an existing technology is being developed. The main difference between microprocessors and computers is cost. The people at Westinghouse have just bought a new microprocessor-based computer: they found that its box had been made unnecessarily large to accord with the cost of the computer.

With computers at the price they were, it very often paid to keep people employed because that was the more economic way of doing it. But with complicated microprocessors, the graph crosses, and it becomes better to employ the machine rather than the person. These wretched chips are going to be producing wealth. In the coming days we have to see that that wealth is distributed in an equitable sort of way. There are many of us who believe that that is not being done at the moment. If you put microprocessors into the equation then there is even less likelihood of it being done. The terrific amount of wealth that they will be producing, with a very much reduced work force, means that we have to see that the wealth is distributed in a correct and equitable way.

When you are on the shop floor in other countries you cannot tell whether your are in this country, the States, the Soviet Union, Czechoslovakia or Hungary, because the production lines all look the same. Basically they are all working with the same sort of equipment. In some of the socialist countries, their equipment is more advanced than ours. But you come to the conclusion that our production is socialist. We do it together. We know how to do it. What we have not learned to do is to socially distribute the profits that are made from it. What the socialist countries are doing whatever may be their weaknesses or their wrongs from one point of view or another, is learning, and learning very rapidly, how to increase the wealth that they make from their increased technology.

Finally, the importance of recruitment, not only where software people are concerned, must be emphasised. If word processing takes on, if the investment is made by the big companies, then with the typewriter being both an input and output terminal, the role of the office worker, the role of filing clerks and all those sort of people will be a lost cause. We have to recruit them before they are there no longer.

# Part 2
# Background Papers

7  Questionnaire

8  The Impact of Computer Technology

9  The Changeover to Electronics

10  The Structure of the Electronics Industry

11  Computer-Aided Administration

12  Computer-Aided Design

13  Computer-Aided Manufacture in Batch Production

# 7 Questionnaire

## National Computer Industry Advisory Panel

This note has been compiled by the Computer Industry Advisory Panel to form a basis for discussion at the TASS Conference on "Computer Technology and Employment". It is based on the TUC's "Industrial Strategy Checklist for Trade Union Representatives".

The TUC General Council have argued that investment in UK manufacturing industry should be doubled between 1978 and 1988. They believe that such an investment effort is essential if the recent decline in the performance of UK manufacturing is to be reversed and a new growth path established.

They calculate that the target of doubling the flow of capital available to UK manufacturing industry will require an annual rate of increase in investment of 7 to 8 per cent per year, and an overall growth in total national output of around 5 per cent per year. If used wisely to finance this manufacturing investment, they believe that the North Sea oil surplus will enable these historically high rates of growth to be achieved and sustained.

Such increases in investment, if they come about, could involve major changes in the organisation of work. New products, many incorporating micro-electronic control, will obsolete existing mechanical and electro-mechanical devices. In parallel with these developments computerisation of design and administration will continue to develop, leading to the devaluation of skills and qualifications and possibly bringing health hazards in its wake.

The questions below are designed to ascertain how far this process has already developed in industry, and the level of control the Union can bring to bear to defend the interests of our members. The debate around them will be used in the updating of the Union's policy on the manufacture and application of computer systems.

**Products**

(i) What rate of growth in demand for the company's products is forecast over the next three, five and ten years?

(ii) Has the company taken into account the likely effect of the North Sea oil revenues on demand?

(iii) What rate of growth of output is the company planning for over the next three, five and ten years?

(iv) Will this growth of output meet the forecast growth in demand for the company's products?

(v) Is the company planning to change the range of products it makes, in particular as a result of technological change? If so, what rate of growth of output is being planned for the new products, and will the old products be run down?

**Investment**

(i) What are the investment plans of the company in the coming three, five and ten year periods?

(ii) What proportion of company profits is spent on Research and Development? Does the company receive any R & D grants from the Government? To what extent is the Union involved in monitoring these expenditures.

(iii) In multinational companies at what level is R & D policy made, and what international trade union involvement is there in formulating policy? Are representatives satisfied that this and other investment taking place abroad would not be more worthwile in the UK.

(iv) What is the scope for bringing forward investment programmes to prepare for increased demand in 1979 and the 1980's.

(v) Has the company considered applying for selective assistance under an Industry Act? Is the company aware of the Government's Selective Investment Scheme and the Product Development Scheme – in particular the Microelectronics Industry Support Plan, and the Microprocessor Application Project?

(vi) What is the age of capital equipment in the company? The TUC has advised Union representatives to press for an inventory in each company and where the average age of plant and machinery is above that of the most efficient 20% of firms they state that there is a prima facia case for new investment. Is this requirement met by the company?

## Manpower

(i) What are the anticipated manpower levels in each EITB category of staff over the next five years?

(ii) To what extent are changes which have taken place, or are about to take place, due to changing product technology? To what extent are they the result of the introduction of computer aided design, administration and production techniques?

(iii) What plans are the company drawing up to ensure the effective employment of its manpower resources? Is it developing new products to utilise the workers existing skills and experiences?

## Education and Training

(i) What steps are the company taking to increase training and retraining, particularly of young people in the light of present and prospective shortages of skilled workers?

(ii) What agreements have been reached concerning regular sabbatical periods for continuing education of existing staff?

## Management and Union Organisation

(i) What procedures exist to control the introduction or upgrading of computer systems, the rationalisation of documentation and standards, and multiple access to technical databanks.

(ii) What information of a personal nature is collected by the company, for example, statistics on current or past performance? Is any of this information collected automatically?

(iii) What procedures exist to control access to personal information?

(iv) What agreements have been reached to monitor the health and safety aspects of visual display units and any speedup in the volume of work arising from the introduction or upgrading of computer equipment.

# 8 Notes on the economic and social impact of computer technology*

**Ian Benson,**
**National Computer Industry**
**Advisory Panel**

## Introduction

This paper examines the road along which computer technology has travelled from the research laboratory to a mass production industry. It looks at the technical, economic and human constraints on its development and at the related question of the management of unemployment. Finally it gives a progress report of the action taken by the European trade union movement in controlling the further development of the technology; in particular within the forum of the National Economic Development Council.

## The Diffusion of Computer Technology

The route from the research laboratory to mass production is never easy in any new technology. The internal combustion engine, which took its present form in 1876, has yet to find its way into the hands of 50% of the population (001). Nuclear energy, a contemporary of the computer, is still in a lengthy development phase.

In comparison the progress of the computer industry has been remarkable. In just 30 years it has developed from nothing to production lines capable of manufacturing 100 000 microcomputers per month. It has consistently exhibited the highest annual productivity growth rate of any

---

*First published as "Computers and the Labour Movement", in Infotech State of the Art Report, "Microcomputer Systems," 1978.

sector of industry and the latest figures suggest that it may have halted the
rapid decline in employment, over 20%, which has taken place since 1970
(see Figure 1).

| Sector | Annual Changes (%) | |
| --- | --- | --- |
| | Output | Employment |
| Petrochemicals | + 4·5 | + 1·5 |
| Drugs | + 11 | − 1·5 |
| Iron and Steel | + 11 | − 1·25 |
| Foundries | + 1·5 | − 3 |
| Electronic Components | + 8·5 | + 1·5 |
| Electronic Computers | + 24·5 | + 2·25 |
| Clothing | + 7·25 | − 1·25 |

Figure 1:   Productivity in major industrial sectors

The manufacture of computers is now an international business which is
well on target to become the third largest in the world by 1980. With the
leading automobile and petrochemical industries about to face severe
problems in the near future, computers may well head the league long
before North Sea oil runs out.

Like those of the internal combustion engine, the roots of the computer
lie in the 19th century. Two English mathematicians, Charles Babbage and
George Boole, carried out the theoretical work which was ultimately
realized in working machines during the Second World War.

Babbage designed two calculating machines, the Difference Engine and
the Analytical Engine, although he failed to construct either owing to
problems with the machining of components. The Difference Engine was
funded by the Admiralty who hoped to use it for the construction of
accurate mathematical tables, but in 1842, after Babbage had spent £17 000
of their money, the Government withdrew support for the project.
Babbage continued to the end of his life with his attempts to implement the
Analytical Engine, on which the design of the modern computer is based.

George Boole made his contribution with the invention of a notation for
describing the function of machines. It is the basis of every computer
programming language.

When the development of the computer resumed during the Second World War attempts were made to implement it, first in electromechanical and then electronic vacuum tube technology. An electromechanical machine, the Automatic Sequential Control Calculator, was developed by IBM at Harvard University for the United States Navy and was rapidly superseded by the Army's vacuum tube ENIAC. Similar machines were constructed in the United Kingdom. Their purpose, like Babbage's machine, was to enable the accurate calculation of mathematical tables and the carrying out of similar numerical tasks. They led to the development of both Numerical Analysis, a new branch of mathematics which broke the solutions of complex equations into sequences of repetitive tasks, and also associated programming languages for describing these tasks.

At the same time electronic technology had developed from vacuum tube to solid state devices, with the introduction of the transistor in 1947. Subsequent advances have all been in the area of the technology for manufacturing these components. Sophisticated techniques for printing on silicon crystals now enable thousands of small transistors to occupy the area which one occupied in 1947. The complex interconnection patterns which linked vacuum tubes and Babbages's mechanical rods can now be printed in one operation.

Programming languages and techniques have not developed at anywhere near the rate of manufacturing technology despite equivalent investment and programming is now regarded as the prime technical constraint on the development of the computer. Despite this problem the range of applications of the machine has expanded enormously, and computers are now found in every sector of the economy (see Figure 2). Since early machines had little capacity to store information they were primarily used for calculating, but with the improvement of external magnetic storage techniques new applications could develop in 'data processing' areas of industry, government and commerce.

Today's pattern of computer use can be divided into those applications which have been standardized and can almost be bought off the shelf and those which are still in the development stage. The standard applications include: payroll processing, sale and stock ledger work, design automation in electrical, mechanical and civil engineering, and automatic assembly and testing of electronic equipment. Still in the development phase are applications of increasing sophistication, linking standard packages such as these, perhaps running on different computers.

Computer-based devices are being developed for the direct collection of data at source, such as electronic cash registers, typewriters, bank tellers,

| STANDARD IND.CLASS-IFICATION | ORDER | 1975 Number | 1975 Percentage |
|---|---|---|---|
| | PRIVATE SECTOR | | |
| 1 | Agriculture, forestry and fishing | 14 | ·1 |
| 11 | Mining and quarrying | 13 | ·1 |
| 111 | Food, drink and tobacco | 352 | 2·6 |
| 1V | Coal and petroleum products | 42 | ·3 |
| V | Chemicals and allied industries | 344 | |
| V1 | Metal manufacture | 109 | |
| V11 | Mechanical engineering | 409 | |
| V11 | Instrument engineering | 123 | |
| 1X | Electrical engineering | 622 | |
| X | Shipbuilding and marine engineering | 36 | |
| X1 | Vehicles | 351 | |
| X11 | Metal goods, not elsewhere specified | 139 | 23 |
| X111 | Textiles | 136 | |
| X1V | Leather, leather goods and furs | 12 | |
| XV | Clothing and footwear | 119 | |
| XV1 | Bricks, pottery, glass, cement, etc | 125 | |
| XV11 | Timber, furniture, etc | 71 | |
| XV111 | Paper, printing and publishing | 328 | |
| X1X | Other manufacturing industries | 117 | |
| XX | Construction | 155 | 1·2 |
| XX1 | Gas, electricity and water | 4 | |
| XX11 | Transport and communications | 726 | 5·5 |
| XX111 | Distributive trades | 761 | 5·7 |
| XX1V | Insurance, banking, finance and business services | 4499 | 34 |
| XXV | Professional and scientific services | 209 | |
| XXV1 | Miscellaneous services | 197 | |
| | PUBLIC SECTOR | | |
| 1 | Central government (included armed services, government departments and research establishments) | 823 | 6·2 |
| 11 | Local government | 573 | 4·3 |
| 111 | Nationalized industry and other public sectors (not including transport): | | |
| | a)  public bodies | 345 | 2·6 |
| | b)  public utilities | 428 | 3·2 |
| | c)  atomic energy | 114 | ·9 |
| | d)  research associations and councils | 175 | 1·3 |
| | e)  educational | 797 | 6 |
| | TOTAL | 13 268 | 100 |

Figure 2:   The distribution of computers in the UK (Source: National Computer Index, April 1975)

and clocking-in cards. Indeed micro-electronic technology has been behind most of the new products of the past ten years (see Figure 3).

| COMMUNICATIONS | MEDICINE |
|---|---|
| • Subscriber trunk dialling | • Body scanners and other advanced diagnostic equipment |
| • Global TV and telephone services by satellite | • Heart pacemakers |
| • Viewdata | • Patient monitoring systems |
| • Push-button telephone dialling | • Computer-produced speech for the vocally impaired |
| • Compact radio telephone systems | • Kidney dialysis equipment |
| • Solid state TV cameras | • Electronic aids and sight for the blind |

| HOME ENTERTAINMENT AND CONSUMER PRODUCTS | DEFENCE |
|---|---|
| • Video games | • Night viewing equipment |
| • Teletext — Ceefax and Oracle | • Microwave blind landing systems |
| • Video cassette recorders | • Battlefield radar |
| • Stereo broadcasting | • Advanced weapon-guidance systems |
| • Electronic calculators and wristwatches | • Infra-red surveillance equipment |
| • Electronic musical instruments | • The cruise missile |

| COMMERCE | MANUFACTURING INDUSTRY |
|---|---|
| • Word processors | • Electronically controlled machine tools |
| • Cash and stock control terminals | • Advanced instrumentation systems |
| • On-line ordering systems | • Electronic measuring equipment |
| • Visual information systems | • Electronic motor speed and temperature control systems |
| • Desk-top computers | • Automated welding |

*Figure 3: Micro-electronic based products 1968-1978*

## Economic Constraints

Developing the technology has required the allocation of vast amounts of capital, and the creation of major markets for the new products. As in Babbage's day it has been the military who have absorbed the bulk of production, and governments have therefore been intimately involved in promoting the development of national industries for strategic reasons.

The UK Ministry of Technology stated in 1968 for example:

"To fail to produce an indigenous industry would expose the country to the possibilities that industrial, commercial, strategic or political decisions made in America could heavily influence our ability to manufacture, to trade, to govern, or to defend; the UK is the only country outside America which has a significant indigenous computer industry capable of development into a world class enterprise. That centres on ICL." (002)

In America, the first major market for computer products, 70% of the Government's computers are used by its military agencies. This has led to the ascendancy of a single company, IBM, which has dominated the world market for over 20 years. Its position grew naturally from its close relationship with the government during the war. At that time 95% of the United States' punch card machines were manufactured by IBM.

The Vietnam war provided a substantial stimulus to the development of the technology. General Westmorland, when in charge of American forces in Vietnam, described the weapons being developed there in these terms:

"On the battlefield of the future, enemy forces will be located, tracked and targeted almost instantaneously through the use of datalinks, computer-assisted intelligence evaluation, and automated fire control." (003)

The purchasing policy of the Government effectively excluded any significant competition to IBM's emergence. The Company attained a commanding technological lead, and as the development of each generation of equipment depended intimately on the previous level of the technology it was able to consolidate its position. The design for a new micro-electronic circuit, for example, is first simulated on a computer. When it is complete:

"The computer itself can prepare the master drawings that will be employed to define the circuit pattern on the silicon. Other computers supervise the fabrication process, and still another one tests the completed chips, automatically marking the defective one." (004)

By its control of technology IBM has been able to regulate the rate of its transfer into production, and hence the speed of obsolescence of its competitors' equipment. Not surprisingly, major companies have been forced to withdraw from the market in recent years; General Electric, RCA and the French CII.

The rapid turn-around in products has given added flexibility, to those companies remaining in the business, over the location of their factories. In Britain most of the US computer companies have located themselves in Scotland to maximize the Government assistance available to them. The jobs which were created have rarely lasted more than ten years, as companies like ITT, Honeywell and NCR have moved on to produce new products in more favourable locations.

As the companies sought to develop markets away from military areas their first targets were the large government and private organisations, who had vast information handling and processing needs.

To sell the new products the manufacturers resorted to the gimmicks of the patent medicine salesman, as Professor James Lighthill noted in his famous report to the Science Research Council on the activities of the so called 'Artificial Intelligence'(AI) scientists. This elite core of academics have received substantial funds over 30 years for largely unsuccessful efforts to build computer based 'robots', language translators, and chess-playing machines, Lighthill noted:

> "The long-term interest of the big international computer manufacturers in bringing about some spectacular achievement of 'machine intelligence' against such a well developed human intelligence as an able chess player, in order to assist in selling more generally their products' potentiality for superceding human intellectual activity, has been an incentive to the devotion of quite considerable resources to producing an effective program." (005)

The AI scientists have been more successful however in keeping alive the anthropomorphic conception of machines, which dates back to the Golem, and nineteenth century automata. Their work has sustained science fiction as a literary form, enabling the 'robot' to strike deep roots in contemporary culture.

Once the large bureaucracies were hooked on the automation of data processing their structure could change so that they could run at far finer margins. The machine has for example enabled stock levels to be set automatically to meet production plans, distribution to be rationalized between warehouses, and production to be optimized between plants. In many companies the complete production and distribution cycle has been linked in this way to create monolithic international enterprises.

The savings achieved by these large organizations have served to undermine the viability of their smaller competitors and thus the process of mergers and takeovers has been accelerated. In this way the computer has contributed towards the increasing concentration of ownership in industry. The share of the hundred largest companies in the nett output of manufacturing industry rose from 15% in 1909 to 20% in 1950, but it had grown to nearly 50% by 1970. It has been calculated that if the current rate of increase continues, their share will reach two-thirds of the total by 1980 (006).

## Human Constraints

These developments have not taken place without causing a reaction from employees, consumers and voters. The introduction of a piece of computer equipment into a factory or office inevitably causes anxiety about short term job prospects. The growth of big Government and big business to which it has contributed has alienated consumers and voters even if it may have led to more efficient administration. This alienation is sufficient to ensure that no Government can feel secure if it allows the closure through bankruptcy of a major organization.

The reaction of employees can be seen in the statistics for trade union growth. The TUC has grown by 50% since the war, to represent almost 12 million employees, despite a massive contraction in employment in its traditional areas, such as railways and mines. As they have grown the unions have sought to mitigate the effects on staff of the introduction of computer machinery, and they have more recently come to question basic assumptions about the employment implications of automation.

TASS for example, which organizes staff in engineering, has doubled in size in seven years to become the largest staff union in the industry. In 1972 the union published guidelines on the use of computer aided design equipment which saw its consequences in terms of the fragmentation of intellectual skills, the intensification of the workrate and an increase in unsocial hours working (007).

Such effects have certainly been seen in industry, perhaps most dramatically in computer staff areas which had the world at their feet not so long ago (008). In the early sixties computer programmers were acknowledged to have highly paid, secure and interesting work. Automation of program writing made possible by more powerful machines has enabled the boundaries of the division of labour in their areas to be redrawn. Now there is the so-called chief programmer team organisation which breaks down programming into a range of designing, coding and testing operations carried out by staff of lower qualification grouped around one or two specialists.

Computer operators too have been affected by the spread of shift working. This is reflected in a substantial shift premium element in their salaries, which have risen by 172% over the last five years compared to the mere 100% rise in programmers' salaries. A survey carried out in West Germany demonstrated that shift working was highly damaging to the individual; the ulcer rate of workers on a rotating shift was 8 times higher than that of other workers. Similar surveys have shown that the divorce rate amongst shift workers is approximately 50% higher than average and the juvenile delinquency rate of their children can often be 80% higher.

Similar examples can be found in all areas in employment. In welding, for example, a manual occupation, there is the growing use of the Unimate 'Robot'. This is programmed by taking a skilled welder who moves the arm of the machine as if it was his welding rod. Once he has carried out this task the machine can repeat it. Although such first generation machines were largely insensitive to the position of the object being welded, with obvious effects on the accuracy of the weld, new machines with sensors to enable the arm to be aligned far more accurately to the object's position have been developed.

Maintenance staff have been affected by the development of telemetry, which enables the central monitoring of remote outstations. Skilled technicians no longer have to be sent out to diagnose faults, and semi-skilled technicians can be sent out to repair machinery, armed with the necessary parts. This leads to the intellectual workload in the centre increasing, while decreasing the number of jobs for skilled men.

A similar pattern has been seen in Engineering Design. Ten years ago structural design, whether of ships, aeroplanes or buildings required qualified engineers to calculate whether the structure would bear the load expected of it. That calculation, both empirical and mathematical, has been internalized in a number of computer programs. They enable the structure to be input, and displayed on a screen on which a curser can be used to apply a simulated load. A spectrum of colour indicates where the stress is building up so that a semi-skilled operator moving a pointer around a screen may now replace a room full of mathematicians.

Even clerical staff who already have routine jobs have had their conditions eroded. We have seen, in data processing, in the last 5 years a growth in the so-called 'twilight shift' operation, that is people working 4 o'clock to 9 o'clock, in the evening. These are generally married women with young children who find it difficult to obtain employment, and by taking work in this way risk similar social consequences to other forms of shift working.

More recently trade union concern has centred on the way in which computer technology has fragmented social relationships at work, a factor which can also lead to stress. The TUC have written in their (009) 'The Trade Union Role in Industrial Policy':

"While the new methods of computer controlled planning systems in data processing offer the prospects of greatly increased productivity they also make it more difficult for the ordinary worker to understand the processes which dictate the pattern and pace of work."

Perhaps this is why the Committee of Engineering Professors in their evidence to the Finniston Committee of Enquiry into the Engineering Profession apparently believe that the career options of really able students at school are increasingly going into medicine, or law, or joining TASS (010).

## The Management of Unemployment

Perhaps the most significant social consequence of the development of microcomputers is the influence it has had on the way in which unemployment is viewed by the trade unions. The European labour movement has become increasingly concerned that electronics may lead to the 1980s becoming an era of mass unemployment, and their concern has prompted discussions at every level of government. Meanwhile as the pattern of employment has altered in response to technological change, unemployment levels have risen, despite government action as shown in Figure 4.

| COUNTRY | UNEMPLOYMENT (%) | | |
| --- | --- | --- | --- |
| | 62-73 | 76 | 77 |
| Canada | 5·3 | 7·2 | 8·1 |
| USA | 4·9 | 7·7 | 7·1 |
| Australia | 1·6 | 4·4 | 5·1 |
| Belgium | 2·1 | 5·8 | 6·4 |
| France | 1·8 | 4·2 | 4·6 |
| West Germany | 1·3 | 4·7 | 4·4 |
| Italy | 3·6 | 3·9 | 4·7 |
| UK | 2·4 | 5·8 | 6·9 |

Figure 4:   Changing levels of unemployment

Until recently the TUC, like many politicians, believed that employment was not threatened by automation and would recover its old levels by traditional methods of economic management. As late as 1965 they could write:

"The contrast between the present day and the position a century ago is dramatic. Any trade unionist at that time with the ability to foresee the technological changes that have taken place in the last century, might well have feared that all the goods and services produced a hundred years ago could have been supplied with modern techniques by a fraction of the 1870 labour force. In fact scientific and technological change has made many new products possible and our requirements have increased at least as fast as industry's ability to meet them."(011)

It now appears that Sir Keith Joseph is alone in holding this view, although it may be shared by the Artificial Intelligence scientist who has just been appointed external technical advisor to his Party on microelectronics (012). According to Sir Keith (013) there is no threat to employment since:

"If that analysis were true, we would be left without any jobs after the industrial revolution, which, instead, increased vastly the wealth of the country and the number of jobs."

The opinion of employers, Government and unions is rather different. The European Metalworkers Federation, which groups Western European engineering unions, recently adopted a document (014) on the development of data processing, which stated:

"The EMF in no way shared the optimism of certain Governments, employers and the European Commission, that the new technologies in the field of informatics will have a favourable effect on the employment situation in general and the number of jobs in particular."

The tri-partite National Economic Development Council (015) reflected this view when it reported in February 1978 that:

"Studies of the electronic industry . . . have shown that the bulk of the expansion in computing into machine tools, telecommunications and office equipment has yet to come. These developments will have serious implications for the demand for maintenance and design staff, in addition to their implications for the career prospects of those working in offices and on production lines."

The Council's call for an early study of the employment implications of microelectronics has been taken up in recent months by a host of bodies including the Government, the Conservative and Labour Parties, and the Friends of the Earth.

The Government have taken the initiative to supplement the on-going work of the NEDC itself by referring the whole question both to the Think Tank and the Prime Minister's Advisory Council for Applied Research. In a significant shift in industrial policy they have endorsed the labour movement's concerns over employment. The Department of Industry, in its recent review of Government Computing Policy (016) stated:

"The human element has received less emphasis than it deserves. NEDC is (perhaps for the first time that this has been done) tackling the question of manpower in computing. There would undoubtedly be a higher return within the computer-using community and within the computer industry to investment in improved education and training leading to greater efficiency in writing of software (now becoming relatively more expensive with the cheaping of hardware and the blurring boundary between the two) and in the operation of computers. In particular the Department wishes to give a decisive push in the re-training of engineers in the use of digital technology based particularly on the microprocessor . . . .

The microprocessor/microcomputer and other achievements in microelectronics are rapidly penetrating many industries where they enable new products or replace mechanical or electromechanical devices or hard-wired electronics. We must help to provide the educational and training or re-training basis to allow these developments to proceed."

It is indeed surprising that Governments of both parties, who have been intimately involved in sponsoring the computer industry, should have apparently overlooked the manpower implications of the technology. Perhaps this is because thay have had to cross the same minefield in devising their strategy as the NEDC (see Figure 5).

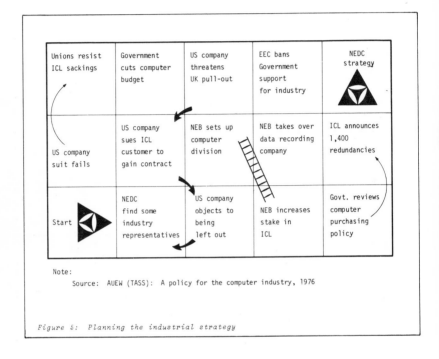

Note:

Source: AUEW (TASS): A policy for the computer industry, 1976

*Figure 5: Planning the industrial strategy*

The changing attitude of the trade union movement which has caused this flurry of activity has been fuelled by the growing realization that the expansion in white collar employment, which partially compensated for the loss of jobs in the manufacturing sector since the war, is now being paralleled by the rapid development of information handling products.

Information handling now represents the biggest single sector of employment and it is still growing rapidly. Figure 6 shows the changes which have taken place in employment despite the turndown in economic activity since 1970. Some of these changes have been a direct result of the development of computer technology which has displaced or sought to displace electrical or mechanical technologies in a whole range of industries. For example, in telecommunications tens of thousands of jobs have been lost in the past few years, while in the newspaper industry, trade unionists have slowed down the introduction of computer based machinery.

*Employed, Male and Female, '000s*

| | CHANGE, 71-74 | CHANGE, 74-76. |
|---|---|---|
| MANUFACTURING | - 181 | - 465 |
|   Engineering | - 55 | - 144 |
|   Metals | - 68 | - 100 |
|   Others | - 58 | - 221 |
| CONSTRUCTION | + 68 | - 69 |
| SERVICES | + 857 | + 360 |
|   Transport | - 62 | - 39 |
|   Distribution | + 152 | - 8 |
|   Insurance | + 139 | + 1 |
|   Professional Services | + 368 | + 261 |
|   Miscellaneous | + 182 | + 42 |
|   Public Sector Services | + 78 | + 103 |
| OTHERS | - 95 | - 38 |
| ALL | + 649 | - 212 |

*Figure 6:  Changing structure of employment in Great Britain, 1971-76*

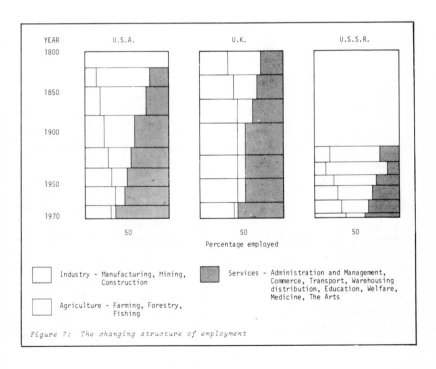

*Figure 7:  The changing structure of employment*

Such a change in the structure of employment has occurred in all advanced industrial countries, as can be seen from Figure 7, which compares the distribution of employment in Britain since 1800 with that in America and Russia. In Britain the growth in white collar areas which has taken place has not been sufficient to help compensate for the decline in the number of manufacturing jobs. Recent years have seen a disturbing rise in unemployment amongst young people who might have expected to have been employed in services. Figure 8 shows that almost 30% of those unemployed are in their twenties.

| MALES | Under 18 | 18-19 | 20-29 | 30-39 | 40-49 | 50-59 | 60 and over |
|---|---|---|---|---|---|---|---|
| 1971 July | 5·0 | 7·1 | 24·9 | 16·0 | 15·2 | 14·7 | 17·0 |
| 1972 January | 4·3 | 6·6 | 26·0 | 17·2 | 15·5 | 14·5 | 15·8 |
| July | 5·2 | 7·0 | 24·9 | 15·8 | 15·0 | 14·8 | 17·4 |
| 1973 January | 4·3 | 6·8 | 24·8 | 15·6 | 14·8 | 15·4 | 18·3 |
| July | 3·5 | 6·1 | 22·6 | 14·5 | 14·6 | 16·5 | 22·1 |
| 1974 January | - | - | - | - | - | - | - |
| July | 4·4 | 6·7 | 25·1 | 15·1 | 13·7 | 15·3 | 19·6 |
| 1975 January | - | - | - | - | - | - | - |
| July | 7·5 | 9·9 | 29·7 | 15·1 | 12·2 | 11·8 | 13·8 |
| 1976 January | 5·9 | 7·4 | 30·3 | 17·2 | 13·3 | 12·6 | 13·4 |
| July | 14·2 | 6·8 | 26·9 | 15·4 | 12·1 | 11·8 | 12·9 |
| 1977 January | 6·1 | 7·0 | 29·8 | 17·5 | 13·2 | 13·0 | 13·4 |
| July | 15·3 | 7·1 | 26·4 | 15·7 | 11·8 | 12·0 | 11·7 |
| | | | | | | | |
| FEMALES | | | | | | | |
| 1971 July | 16·0 | 14·8 | 29·5 | 9·2 | 12·5 | 17·4 | 0·6 |
| 1972 January | 15·2 | 15·1 | 30·7 | 9·4 | 12·1 | 17·1 | 0·5 |
| July | 16·3 | 15·7 | 31·3 | 8·8 | 11·1 | 16·3 | 0·4 |
| 1973 January | 14·0 | 16·8 | 32·0 | 8·8 | 11·1 | 16·8 | 0·4 |
| July | 11·5 | 15·6 | 33·4 | 8·8 | 11·0 | 19·2 | 0·4 |
| 1974 January | - | - | - | - | - | - | .- |
| July | 13·0 | 17·0 | 34·3 | 8·7 | 10·0 | 16·5 | 0·5 |
| 1975 January | - | - | - | - | - | - | - |
| July | 19·2 | 20·7 | 33·4 | 8·0 | 8·1 | 10·3 | 0·4 |
| 1976 January | 18·0 | 16·8 | 33·8 | 9·9 | 9·4 | 11·7 | 0·4 |
| July | 32·8 | 13·8 | 27·6 | 8·3 | 7·8 | 9·3 | 0·3 |
| 1977 January | 16·7 | 16·1 | 35·2 | 10·6 | 9·6 | 11·3 | 0·4 |
| July | 31·4 | 14·3 | 28·7 | 8·8 | 7·7 | 8·8 | 0·3 |

Figure 8:   Percentage of total number unemployed by age

Despite the deployment of increasing numbers of computers, white collar areas remain the least capitalised sector of employment. Indeed by international standards the density of computer use in the UK is only moderate (Figure 9). In general the equipment available to office workers, a telephone or a typewriter, is insignificant compared with the machinery available to manual workers engaged in production. This position is rapidly changing however since it is already cheaper to store and transmit information electronically than by any other means. The semiconductor manufacturers have calculated that by 1985 very little of their production of microcomputers can be absorbed by either automation systems or through the development of consumer products. Even if every home has ten control systems, such as washing machines, which contain micro-processors this would only absorb 10% of their production. Their only available mass market is information handling products.

Reflecting these developments the Post Office, reviewing its services to the end of the century, anticipates that office automation will be the major area of expansion. From 1980 to 1990 they envisage the development of centre to centre close circuit television, the TV display of dialled data banks, the use of audio-visual telephones, of very cheap facsimile terminals and of fast upper and lower telex. These services will be additional to those for the remote control of plant and machinery and the reading of meters. In the last decade of the century they plan the development of electronic mail and the home printing of electronically transmitted newspapers (017).

| Country | 1975 | | end 1976 | |
| | Population (millions) | GNP ($ billions) | Number of computers installed | Number of computers installed per million people |
| --- | --- | --- | --- | --- |
| USA | 208·8 | 1355·5 | 165 000 | 790 |
| FRANCE | 51·7 | 302·8 | 16 100 | 311 |
| GERMANY | 61 7 | 390 5 | 18 800 | 304 |
| CANADA | 21·9 | 136·9 | 6 200 | 283 |
| UNITED KINGDOM | 55·8 | 176·0 | 14 400 | 258 |
| JAPAN | 107·0 | 449·0 | 31 000 | 244 |
| SCANDINAVIA | 21·8 | 140·2 | 5 200 | 238 |
| BENELUX | 23·3 | 128·2 | ·5 300 | 227 |
| ITALY | 54·4 | 142·8 | 7 700 | 141 |

Figure 9:   Computers installed by population and GNP (Source:    EDP Industry Report)

## Towards a National Plan

Technological change, like poverty, is always thrown into sharp relief at times of mass unemployment. With the Manpower Services Commission predicting a shortfall of 2 million jobs by 1981, the development of the microcomputer has inevitably has political consequences. The labour movement while pressing ahead with the development of the National Enterprise Board, has put renewed vigour into its demands for continuing education and social ownership.

Since the Industrial Revolution workers have resisted technological change where it threatened their chances of employment, and this resistance has had a profound effect on political life. The introduction of the factory system at the turn of the 19th century met with resistance on both economic and moral grounds. Followers of General Ludd, who was known as the 'Redresser' had considerable public support. Although their opposition is often simply painted as resistance to the use of machinery, as E P Thompson notes in 'The making of the English Working Class' (018):

"What was at issue was the 'freedom' of the capitalist to destroy the customs of the trade, whether by new machinery, by the factory system, or by unrestrictive competition, beating down wages, undercutting his rivals, and undermining standards of craftsmanship."

Although the Luddites were eventually defeated in their campaign of direct action to resist the spread of the factory system, their activities were indirectly an influence of the widening of the franchise and a century of progressive legislation on the formation of trade unions and the regulation of conditions of employment.

These advances were not won without a sustained struggle. Trade unions were illegal until 1824, while contemporary wages were subsistence level and the only limit to working hours was physical exhaustion. In 1836 the 60 hour week and extra payment for overtime was won, and in 1871 another great struggle reduced the working week to 54 hours. It was not until 1898 after an unsuccessful battle for an 8 hour day, that the Amalgamated Society of Engineers, predecessors of the AUEW, won the right to negotiate for its members. Not until 1919 was the working week reduced to 47 hours and recognition by employers obtained for local representatives.

Those who talk of the 'leisure society' of the future should not under-estimate the magnitude of the battles ahead. The CBI has already indicated its total opposition to the TUC's 35 hour week campaign. A similar reaction can be expected to other essential claims for sabbatical periods, early retirement and increased real earnings. All of these are necessary to raise the level of economic activity, and enable employees to develop their careers.

The computer industry itself has not been backward in debating such policies, in response to its own manpower problems. The NEDC has published best practice standards for paid training in the industry, and recommend unions and employers to negotiate schemes at this level (Figure 10). TASS believes that in order to compensate for the over-specialization demanded by employers and the educational system staff should be free to control the use of this time themselves.

| EITB Category of Staff | Man Hrs./per annum |
|---|---|
| Managerial | 40 |
| Scientists/technologists | 95 |
| Technicians | 160 |
| Administrative and Professional | 45 |
| Clerical and other Office Staff | 20 |
| Supervisors | 25 |
| Craftsmen | 140 |
| Operators | 10 |
| Note: Source: Survey by Computer Manpower Sub-Committee, NEDC. | |

Figure 10: Best practice training schemes in the computer industry

To meet the growing need for technical training and re-training which will be created, TASS has called for the Engineering Industry Training Board (EITB) to be developed, through the Manpower Services Commission, into the major centre for setting training standards and co-ordinating the provision of courses. The detailed programme is set out in the union's evidence to the Finniston Enquiry (019). This viewpoint is shared by the NEDC who called for the EITB to 'expand its programme of training of computer staff and technicians' (020). The board has responded positively by agreeing to review their activities in this area, in particularly the provision of appreciation courses for managers on microelectronics (021).

In parallel with the EITB the trade union movement is developing its own training programmes on the implications of computer technology, using the time-off provisions of the Employment Protection Act. These courses are aimed at assisting union representatives to negotiate the design of computer systems. The TUC is already looking closely at experience in Norway where a National Agreement has been reached with the Employers' Federation which gives trade unions not only the right to all relevant information about systems which may affect their interests, but the right to nominate and train representatives to participate in systems design, with an implied right of veto.

Although these policies are aimed at increasing the real living standards of all work people they depend intimately on the level of control the labour movement can exert over economic activity, in particular in the manufacturing sector. TUC policy towards manufacturing is based on the Confederation of Shipbuilding and Engineering Unions 'Plan for Engineering'. Although major parts of the plan, notably the public ownership of Shipbuilding and Aerospace, have been carried out by the Government, the policy for the computer industry is still unimplemented. This was formulated in 1972 when a paper (022) presented by TASS was adopted. The paper stated:

"If we accept that the computer industry has the overall importance that is claimed, then the idea of meaningful social and economic planning requires social ownership of the industry."

This policy was updated in 1976 to take account of the technological change which was rapidly merging the computer, telecommunications and electronics industries (023). In a comprehensive programme designed to secure the skills and the products which will be required in the 80s the union called for the strengthening of the UK indigenous industry centred on ICL by the establishment of component manufacturing facilities and the public ownership of the fragmented software industry through the National Enterprise Board.

| COMPANY | ANNUAL SALES | MAJOR PRODUCTS |
|---|---|---|
| *More than 50% holding* | | |
| British Leyland | 2602 | Vehicles, Mechanical Handling Equipment |
| Rolls Royce | 703·9 | Aero-engines |
| Ferranti | 125·4 | Defence Electronics |
| Herbert | 54·3 | Machine Tools |
| Data Recording Instrument Co | 12·0 | Computer Peripherals |
| Sinclair Radionics | 4·2 | Consumer Electronics |
| Systems Programming Holdings | 3·67 | Computer Programs |
| Mollart Engineering Co | 1·95 | Machine Tools |
| Keland Electrics | ·70 | Electrical Machinery |
| Thwaites and Reed | ·12 | Time-recording Machines |
| Bull Motors | New Company | Lift Automation |
| INSAC Data Systems | New Company | Computer Programs |
| *Less than 50% holding* | | |
| Agemaspark | 3·06 | Advanced Machine Tools |
| Aqualisa Products | New Company | Domestic Water Control Systems |
| British Tanners Products | 38·5 | Clothing Manufacturing |
| Cambridge Instruments Co | 17·54 | Electronic-beam Instruments |
| H R Chapman | 1·05 | Sea Surveys, by remote controlled submersibles |
| Computer Analysts and Programmers Holdings | 6·50 | Computer Programs |
| Hydraroll | under ·25 | Mechanical Handling Equipment |
| ICL | 418·6 | Computers |
| Mayflower Packaging | ·42 | Automatic Packaging Equipment |
| North East Audio | Merged Company | Cassette Recorders |
| Packmet International | ·59 | Paper and Board Machinery |
| Pitcraft | 1·93 | Coal-Face Mining Equipment |
| Sandicare Electrics | ·69 | Electronic Control Systems |
| Systime | 4·25 | Small Computers |
| Twinlock | 22·54 | Office Machinery |
| *Companies added since end of Financial Year* | | |
| Fairey Engineering Holdings | – | Parts for nuclear industry, filters and power launches. Aerial Surveys. |
| United Medical Enterprises International | – | Project Management for Hospital Construction |
| Systems Designers International | – | Computer Programs |
| Power Dynamics | – | Hydraulic Tube Manufacturing Equipment |
| Automation and Technical Services (Holdings) | – | Telemetry and Telegraph Equipment |
| Computer and Systems Engineering | – | Message Switching Equipment |

*Figure 11: NEB shareholdings*

This position was largely endorsed by the NEDC. The Council stated that it was:

"Greatly concerned that the manpower and training implications of this diffusion of computer technology should be properly planned. It was also concerned that the development of these new products seems to be taking place largely outside the UK and that this further weakens the infrastructure of the UK computer industry. In particular (it felt) that the manpower requirements of the computer manufacturing and telecommunications industry should be more closely related and that the future of these industries could only be secured by their working more closely together in both their product planning and technical standards."

Certain steps in the required direction have already been taken. The NEB has substantially enlarged its holdings in software companies and taken shares in other small businesses threatened by the development of microelectronics (Figure 11). It has also recently taken a welcome initiative in establishing a £50 million facility for the manufacture of advanced microelectronic components. Nevertheless the major part of union policy, the integration of the telecommunications computer and component industries under public ownership has still to be won.

In every advanced industrial country, government has had to become intimately involved in the development of the computer industry. The trade union movement has called for the support that is given to the industry to be democratically accountable through social ownership. Only if we can secure an advanced computer based industry on this basis can we develop the necessary manpower plans, through collective bargaining and industrial democracy, to ensure that the social consequences of the microcomputer revolution are beneficial.

## References

001 AUEW (TASS)
    *The British motor vehicle industry – a trade union response to the Government white paper*
    (1976)

002 MINISTRY OF TECHNOLOGY
    Evidence received by the Select Committee on Science and Technology
    Sub-Committee D HC 272
    (Session 1969/70)

003 WESTMORLAND W
    Reported in the US Congressional Record
    (Nov 1969)

004 HOTTON W C
    *The large-scale integration of microelectronic circuits*
    Scientific American
    (Sept 1977)

005 LIGHTHILL J
    *Artificial Intelligence*
    Science Research Council
    (1973)

006 PRAIS S J
    National Institute of Economic and Social Research
    Financial Times
    (March 1973)

007 AUEW (TASS)
*Computer aided design – its*
*nature and implications*
(1972)

008 LARKCOM J
*Careers – the money's in*
*computers*
Observer (July 1967)

009 TRADES UNION
CONGRESS
*The trade union rôle in*
*industrial policy*
(1977)

010 SHERCLIFF A
Computer Weekly
(June 1978)

011 TRADES UNION
CONGRESS
*Automation and*
*technological change*
(1965)

012 JOSEPH K
Computer Weekly
(April 1978)

013 *Computernews*
Computer Weekly
(June 1978)

014 EUROPEAN
METALWORKERS
FEDERATION
*Position on the European*
*data processing industry*
*and its use*
(1977)

015 NATIONAL ECONOMIC
DEVELOPMENT
COUNCIL ELECTRONIC
COMPUTERS SECTOR
WORKING PARTY
MANPOWER
SUB-COMMITTEE
*Interim Report*
NEDDY Books (1978)

016 DEPARTMENT OF
INDUSTRY
*Policy for computing*
EUROCOMP '78

017 POST OFFICE REVIEW
COMMITTEE
(CARTER COMMITTEE)
Report (1977)

018 THOMPSON E P
*The making of the English*
*working class*
Gollanz (1963)

019 AUEW (TASS)
*Qualified engineers – the*
*way forward*
Submission to the
Committee of Enquiry into
the Engineering Profession
(1978)

020 NATIONAL ECONOMIC
DEVELOPMENT
COUNCIL
*op cit*

021 ENGINEERING
INDUSTRY TRAINING
BOARD
*Response to the Interim
Report of the Manpower
Sub-Committee of the
Electronic Computer Sector
Working Party*
(May 1978)

022 AUEW (TASS)
*The computer industry*
Confederation of
Shipbuilding and
Engineering Unions (1973)

023 AUEW (TASS)
*A policy for the computer
industry: the NEDC
computer industry strategy –
a trade union response*
(1976)

# 9 The changeover to electronics

## Labour Research Department

### Introduction

The changeover to electronics is already happening. 30 years after the first computer was introduced its descendants the microprocessors are cheaply available.

This paper looks at some cases of employment changes in the past and gives a list of products each with potential employment effects for the future. Although the list does not claim to be more than a collection of some of the more recently announced products the implications for employment are obvious. Unfortunately there is little reason to believe from the history of employment in computers and electronic components that the development of new industries will automatically offset this loss of jobs. An answer to the problems posed by the changeover to electronics which leaves the solution to the job creating effects of supposed new industries is no answer at all.

### Effects on employment

The precise effect that the changeover to electronics will have on employment are not yet known. Studies are being carried out to try and assess the overall impact of these new technologies, but there is growing evidence which suggests that the final result may be a net loss of jobs.

Three different aspects of the effects of the changeover to electronics on employment can be considered:

(i) employment within the electronics industry.
(ii) employment within the industries adopting the new technologies.
(iii) the indirect effects that changing technology has on the competitiveness of companies and countries.

### Employment within the electronics industry

The growth of the electronics industry has seen the rapid development of new products, electronic components being added to existing products and increased applications for both. This is a process which is likely to continue. Not unnaturally these developments, which have created entire new industries, such as the electronic calculator industry, have produced new jobs. It is sometimes suggested that they will create sufficient new employment to offset the loss of jobs caused by the changeover to electronics in other industries. The limited available evidence does not support this view particularly as the development of new products is generally accompanied by the development of new production techniques which require less labour.

For example, employment trends in the computer industry are not encouraging. In the early 1960s computer staff and especially programmers, were in great demand. But the very technology developed by the computer industry has altered the industry's labour requirements. Computers are being developed which can diagnose malfunctions, thereby reducing the skills required of electronic engineers. Automation has been introduced into program writing, again downgrading the skills required of programmers. And, of course, automation and mass production on the manufacturing side have reduced labour requirements. Employment in computer manufacturing in the United Kingdom almost doubled between 1959 and 1971, thereafter declined considerably, reaching a stable level in 1976. (see Table 1)

Table 1          *Employment in computer manufacturing*

| Year | 1959 | 1971 | 1974 | 1975 | 1976 | 1977* |
|---|---|---|---|---|---|---|
| No. of employees | 27,000 | 53,000 | 46,000 | 45,000 | 43,000 | 43,000 |

*estimate

Source: NEDC Electronic Computers Sector Working Party
Manpower Subcommittee Interim Report

A recent survey of computer manufacturing companies undertaken by the Manpower sub-committee of the NEDC Electronic Computers Sector Working Party, showed that the major UK companies expected to increase their labour force by about 11 per cent between 1977 and 1980.

Another NEDC report on electronic components similarly indicates a decline in employment in the industry since reaching a peak of 153,300 in 1974. (Table 2)

Table 2

*Employment in the electronic components industry 1972-77 (GB)*

| Year (at June) | 1972 | 1973 | 1974 | 1975 | (May) 1976 | 1977* |
|---|---|---|---|---|---|---|
| No. of employees | 126,800 | 136,000 | 153,300 | 128,400 | 123,000 | 129,000 |

*estimate

Source: NEDC Electronic Components Sector Working Party
  Progress Report 1978

Employment projections for this industry are less optimistic than for computer manufacture, and depend on the level of output and rate of productivity achieved by the industry. The NEDC report states that output must rise by at least 15 per cent a year merely for employment to remain stable at its present level of 130,000

An important factor affecting the future of both these industries will be the extent to which UK firms will succeed in competing internationally with new products and in the new markets being created. There is no doubt that the new markets are there, and that demand for new products in these fields is growing. However the rate of growth estimated to be needed to *maintain* employment in components, 13 per cent a year, indicates that substantial increase in jobs in these industries is unlikely.

The telecommunications industry itself falls into a rather different category. At least in the UK, although not in a country such as Saudi Arabia, electronic equipment is being introduced as a replacement for electro-mechanical equipment. And this changeover will lead to less need for labour both for maintenance and manufacture. (The effects this will have are detailed in the following section) In time, however, the additional services offered by an all-electronic system may create additional employment. In the UK at least there is no sign of this yet.

### Employment in the industries adopting new technologies

In manufacturing employment can be affected by changes in both product and production technique. Examples of product change are the move from mechanical watches to electronic watches, or the replacement of mechanically operated adding machines by electronic calculators. Examples of changes in production technique are the introduction of robot welding or machine tools controlled by micro processors. However, it is artificial to look at these changes in isolation from each other. Product changes are inevitably associated with changes in production techniques.

The employment changes which occur are either a loss of jobs or a deskilling of the jobs which remain or, most frequently both.

It is extremely difficult to quantify the number of jobs lost due to the introduction of electronic devices. Looking at any particular industry, the employment situation of the past ten years cannot be isolated from the general economic climate of that period. However, it is still instructive to consider particular cases.

One example is in telecommunications. The introduction of stored programme control exchanges affects employment within the telecommunications authority. The experience of Bell Telephone Company in the USA showed that maintenance was reduced by half and manpower productivity was doubled as a result of centralised maintenance. As well as being easily maintained electronic exchange equipment requires less labour to manufacture. A report by M V Posner on Post Office orders for telephone communications switching equipment (Report to the Secretary of State for Industry, May 1977) indicated that the manufacture of £1 million of electromechanical equipment would employ 160 people for a year, compared with 80 for the same value of semi-electronic equipment. Employment in the supplying industry has already fallen from a peak of 91,100 in 1971 to 56,800 in 1977. However a substantial part of this fall was caused by cuts in the Post Office ordering programme for exchange equipment. The experience of a Swedish company L M Ericsson, a major Western European exporter of telephone equipment, has been that, despite an increase in orders for its new exchanges, assembly employment in Sweden fell from 15,300 in mid-1975 to 10,300 in mid-1978. The company still manufactures some electromechanical equipment, so the fall in employment as a result of technical change is still incomplete. The company estimates that in total the workforce will be halved.

Another well known example where jobs have been lost is the watch industry. As the Financial Times commented:

"There can hardly be a more dramatic example of how new technology transforms and entire industry – and the jobs of the people who work in it – than the Swiss watch industry." (12.9.78)

The demand for quartz (electronic) watches has fundamentally altered the watch and clock making industries. On the one hand demand for traditional products has declined, and on the other manufacture of electronic devices has transformed the methods of production in the industry.

The clock industry in South West Germany has slumped, because of competition from electronic timepieces and employment has dropped from 32,000 at the start of the 1970s to 18,000. In Switzerland, where the industry has kept pace with the demand for electronic watches, employment has dropped by about 40 per cent over 8 years, to a current level of 55,000. The majority of employees in the industry are now semi-skilled machine operators, like the 16 workers in a Swiss factory who together control 400 machines which cut teeth for watch parts.

Many examples of the de-skilling effects of the changeover to electronics exist. One case is the UK textile industry which has been the subject of a study by the Science Policy Research Unit at Sussex University (The Impact of Microelectronics on the UK by J M McLean & H J Rush, June 1978). They conclude that:

"At the same time that the use of electronic control systems have facilitated, and in some respects made possible, overall increases in productivity, electronics have also made significant contributions to the progressive removal of the need for craft skills in the process of textile manufacture and to the almost total de-skilling of the production process."

McLean and Rush point out that since the Second World War the textile industry has experienced an accelerating pace of technical change, which has enabled labour productivity to rise 314 per cent in 23 years, from £616 net output per person in 1960 to £1,934 in 1973. Against a background of declining share of the world market, the net result has been a loss of jobs in the industry, falling from 581,200 employed in the textile sector in 1971 to 479,000 in 1976. They illustrate the changeover with two innovations – computer controlled double jaguard knitting machine, which requires the same labour but reduces the time needed to change a pattern from 3-4 hours to a few minutes. And by an electric mill-monitoring system which enables a single weaver to supervise a large number of looms without reducing the quality of cloth produced.

In services banking is an industry which has traditionally been labour intensive, and which has and will continue to introduce labour saving devices. Commercial banking in Britain has grown enormously, and the amount of money 'lent' to the four major clearing banks in current, deposit and other accounts has risen from £27,000 million in 1972 to £61,099 million in 1976. Between 1971 and 1976 employment in the whole sector of "banking and bill discounting" fell from 315,600 in 1971 to 263,000 in 1976. The introduction of the computer has had a tremendous impact of banking, and has reduced the labour required by banks considerably. Now the banks are turning to automated services for customers, which will further reduce the staff employed.

Up to now, the changeover to electronics in the service sector has been concentrated in large organisations. But microprocessors raise the possibility of even small offices bing able to contemplate automation; with the electronic handling of paperwork by word processors. A West German study by Siemens, suggests that by 1990 40 per cent of present office work could be carried out by computerised equipment, and trade unions have calculated that this means a threat to the jobs of 2 million of West Germany's 5 million typists and secretaries.

Below are examples of new products which are likely to affect employment.

### Indirect effect of the changeover

New technology, and in particular microelectronic systems, are being introduced on a worldwide scale, and the competitive position of any particular industry and thus the degree to which it can provide jobs will partly depend on the extent to which it has taken advantage of the higher productivity of new systems. A recent report suggests that UK industry has been slow to adopt new technology compared with foreign enterprises (SPRU June 1978). This has also been recognised by the Government, who in July introduced a scheme to encourage UK industry to apply microprocessor techniques to a wide range of products and processes.

The following are a sample of a few of the latest products being marketed or designed. They are grouped under 4 broad headings, according the the function which they fulfil. The examples do not represent the importance of particular developments, but rather those which have been marketed in the past few months.

### *Design*

#### KITCHENS BY COMPUTER

It has been estimated that it takes ten hours to design the average kitchen and, with the introduction of a microprocessor which, it is claimed, can do the same work as a kitchen designer, this time can be reduced to as little as half an hour.

A housewife should now be able to take her kitchen's measurements to her local dealer where a design can be drawn up on a television screen. Discussions can take place with a designer and modifications instantly made.

Once all the various units have been placed, the machine can show the side elevation of the layout and then produce a contract of sale, an order for part from a supplier, or for the kitchen planner a stockroom, and technical drawings of the kitchen for the installer.

*(Financial Times 4.9.78)*

#### MANAGING DESIGN OF COMPLEX PIPEWORK

A software package called PDMS that is claimed to be far in advance of anything else in the world has been devised. It has been evolved for the design of pipe layouts by process plant contractors and smaller organisations that supply engines, coolers, pipework and other plant components.

"It is much more than an automatic pencil," says Dr Pike. "It is a complete design management package."

PDMS allows the designer or engineer to construct three dimensional representations of every item of plant, down to the level of flanges and gaskets. All the information is stored in memory. On the graphics side, the user can specify the view he want from any angle, and direction and at any eye level. There are facilities for rotation of the image on the screen and for hidden line presentations, with any specified details removed so that particular aspects of the plant layout can be examined on an uncluttered screen.

However, a major benefit is a non-graphics reporting capability. Data on every component in the plant can be recalled in almost any combination or format for use in costing and materials ordering

"It means, for example," explains Dr Pike, "that information on a plant design can be stored in a convenient magnetic form and the, years later if need be, a plant manager can use it to locate components that require replcement or overhaul or to modify the layout for expansion or to take account of a new process."

*(Financial Times 17.7.78)*

## Administration

### TELECOMMUNICATIONS

A breakthrough in the transmission of speech by wire or radio, which may mean that telephone transmission systems could be marketed at a tenth their present cost, has been made by Brigadier Reg King, director of Army telecommunications in the Ministry of Defence. Indications are that this development could also mean that present telephone systems will be able to cope with four or five times their present traffic through the same number of lines

In Brigadier King's system, speech patterns are reduced, with the aid of computers, into a small number of basic shapes, then reconstructed at the receiving end.

*(Financial Times 21.7.78)*

### AUTOMATED MANAGER

A driverless vehicle primarily intended for distributing goods and mail in offices, computer centres, hospitals and industrial complexes has been introduced to the UK. Using automatically detachable containers of various configurations, each battery powered unit is capable of transporting 200 kilos at 30 metres a minute and travels along programmed routes through corridors, offices, workshops etc halting at predetermined positions. Control is achieved by a microprocessor which stores all route programmes and its most important feature is said to be the simplicity of installation.

*(Financial Times 23.8.78)*

SOLICITORS' ACCOUNTS AUTOMATED

Precedent, a computer system for solicitors is being offered by Altergo Computers for client accounting, time recording, word processing and automated production of legal documents.

Precedent 1 is tailored for the smaller practice with up to three thousand "Matters" and is provided on Altergo's microcomputer, the Formula 1. Precedent 2 is able to handle 20,000 matters or more. This system is based on the Avenger mini computer.

Both systems provide comprehensive client matter accounting which can be tailored to individual needs. It gives, for example, draft billing; instant enquiry to matter details; accounts posting; nominal ledger, Full recording for both chargeable and non chargeable time is possible to ensure that accurate charges are calculated for each matter. The fee earner fills out a normal time sheet and details from this are keyed into the system which will then calculate charges from the fee-earners standard and priority rates.

Precedent 2 system has the additional facility to enable "mark sense" cards to be read. With this capability fee-earners simply "tick the box" on a time card. For the larger practice with many transactions this is a cost-effective and simple method of time recording.

(*Financial Times 9.8.78*)

AUTOMATED RESTAURANTS

In place of the traditional cash register Wimpey's modernised restaurant in Notting Hill Gate, London, now has computer controlled Documentor management information systems. Handwritten bills and mental arithmetic are now eliminated and assistants are no longer required to remember prices. The terminals have item keys corresponding to individual menu items which when pressed tell the system exactly what the customer ordered. Using its internal memory the machine prints out a complete descriptive bill, recalling prices, calculating totals, and applying VAT where appropriate.

Throughout the day, AM Documentor maintains a raw product stock record, keeping a tally of what has been sold and how many. At a later date, a communication modem will be added to the system to allow data transfer with a central computer after hours.

(*Financial Times 26.7.78*)

RUNNING A HOTEL BY COMPUTER

First installation of a computerised hotel management system called CHAMPS, has been made at the Penta Hotel in London.

CHAMPS stands for "computerised hotel accounting and management processing system" and makes use of a series of software modules that can be easily tailored and later modified by the user to meet the requirements of a particular hotel. Marcol emphasises that unlike many hotel systems there is no question of the management and staff having to alter their way of working to suit the machine

The Penta installation makes use of a pair of Data General Eclipse S130 computers connected to 15 visual display terminals installed in the reception desks, cashier's areas, accounts office and the housekeeper's office. There are also five associated Tally printing terminals

As each guest arrives his data is entered into the store via the keyboard on the VDU and the display will show a room to meet his needs (although if he rejects it another will be produced). The display can be made to show the status of any room at any time.

A guest's bill is automatically incremented in the store as his stay progresses; at the Penta a somewhat unusual feature in the coupling of a Tiger telephone monitoring system and the drink dispensers in the rooms. Guests can make calls from their rooms without going through the operator, or take a drink, and the cost is automatically accounted for.

At check-out a detailed account is available within seconds.

For management, CHAMPS is able to produce various listings and analyses. For example, it can periodically show the sources of business attracted to the hotel, or give a breakdown of the nationality of guests. Other details the system will provide include an analysis of commissions payable to travel agents, a credit limit list of guests and a daily accounting of all hotel business.

*(Financial Times 7.7.78)*

## Production and Distribution

RETRIEVAL OF MANY PARTS

At one of the key plants involved in the production of the "Tornado" multi-role combat aricraft at the Preston works of British Aerospace, a fully automated system for storing and retrieving small parts is now in operation, called Conserv-a-trieve . . .

The fully automated system has replaced, and combined into one, two existing stores previously in separate locations. The vacated floor area amounted to 10,350 sq ft – the new automated store occupies an area of 4,180 sq ft, a saving of nearly 60 per cent.

Four of the newly introduced machines handle a total of 22,000 parts for the Tornado fighter, and a further 10,000 standard parts for other British Aerospace aircraft, such as the Jaguar tactical strike fighter, the Lightning fighter and the Provost jet trainer.

The components range from bulk-head frames down to the smallest rivets. The largest is 42 in × 15 in high and the weight limit is 300 lb. The entire store consists of about 6,000 containers 6, 9 and 12 in high, and the largest size of bin can hold parts up to 18 in in height.

The machine consists of facing banks of storage containers which rise as high as the building allows. An electrically-controlled mini-load stacker runs between the banks and is directed to the required position by an operator using a simple keyboard which has a five figure location number.

According to the co-ordinates entered on the keyboard, a platform on the stacker travels to the appropriate vertical position and the stacker itself to the horizontal. An extraction device pulls the container on to the platform for delivery to the picking station.

The average time taken to retrieve and return a container is 47 seconds, and the current transaction rate is estimated to be 1,140 operations per man per week, compared with the old storage rate of 972 per man/week, and increase of 17 per cent per man.

*(Financial Times 31.8.78)*

DATA IS EASILY DERIVED

Whessmatic 60 is a device for measuring and displaying the average temperature of liquid products flowing through pipelines . . . Average temperature of liquid products is an important part of the data required for stock inventory requirements at oil storage depots, terminals and refineries. Often the method deployed in obtaining this information is cumbersome and inaccurate as readings are usually taken manually, logged individually and later averaged. Temperature compensated flow meters, on the other hand, will correct volume throughput against temperature, but the information may be lost as there is no provision for recording the data.

The Whessoe unit provides a simple method of obtaining an accurate and permanent record of average temperature and the information can be fed directly to a computer, if desired. It has a temperature transducer, flow input pulser and processor display unit . . .

*(Financial Times 13.7.78)*

KEEPS THE SHIRTS MOVING

A mechanised handling system for the continuous movement of products through the warehouse, on to packaging and up to the higher level despatch bay, has been put into operation at the distribution centre of British Van Heusen, Taunton, Somerset . . .

Some 180,000 dozen shirts are handled each year, of which more than 20 per cent are exported, and in addition to its own output the distribution centre also processes shirts from its outlying production units. These arrive in single boxes for holding in the 20,000 square foot single-storey warehouse where, after checking and classifying, they are placed in a gravity storage system.

Orders are made up and shirts loaded on to wheeled trolleys each of which can hold 120 boxes. The trolleys are then engaged with the carriers of the overhead conveyor which follows a circuit of some 120 yards around the warehouse area.

The conveyor, from the Gough Econ Super 8 range, is said to be a highly adaptable multi-unit dual direction system which can be used for overhead suspension, floor mounting or in-floor installations. Suitable for light, medium and heavy duty applications, it is capable of carrying loads of up to 240 lbs.

Apart from the benefits of consistently moving stick through the adoption of mechanised techniques, the system reduces the element of man handling formerly required, so releasing labour, says the company, for more productive activities which is of especial value during seasonal pressures.

*(Financial Times 25.7.78)*

EXPERIMENTAL MECHANICAL ASSEMBLER DESIGNED

Scientists at IBM have designed an experimental mechanical assembler system that can be programmed to do many different tasks. The system was designed for a medium-volume assembly line, which typically produces several thousand units a year of a particular object. Most assembly line operations fall into this range.

The system consists of a computer-controlled arm and gripping mechanism, equipped with sensors, plus the programming – or software – to direct the movements of the mechanism. The system  capable of assembling kitchen items like blenders and toasters, or office products such as typewriters, staplers and keyboards.

The arm and gripper can be positioned accurately to within a tolerance of .125 mm. Experiments have demonstrated that the machine can put together a typewriter sub-assembly of 8 parts in about 45 seconds.

*(IBM Research Highlights October 1977)*

TELEPHONE EXCHANGE EQUIPMENT

The number of factory man years of labour required to produce a telephone exchange of given capacity is much lower for semi-electronic equipment (known as TXE4) than it is for electro-mechanical equipment (such as Strowger or Crossbar). About 160 man years of labour input are required to produce £1 million worth of Strowger equipment, and perhaps as little as 80 man years to produce £1 million worth of TXE4 equipment; moreover, the overall costs over the whole of its life of a TXE4 exchange of given capacity is markedly less than its Strowger equivalent. Technical progress in this industry is dramatically fast, and the new capital equipment costs less to operate.

(*Post Office Orders for Telecommunication Switching Equipment Report to the Secretary of State for Industry May 1977*)

### CUT STEERED BY MICRO

A flame cutting machine has been developed which makes use of a microprocessor to program and control accurate cuts in pipes up to 1200 mm in diameter. The company maintains that many pipe processing shops still use manual flame cutting methods which, apart from giving inaccurate results consume a,great deal of time and demand great skill and dexterity if quality is to be maintained.

(*Financial Times 28.8.78*)

### CHEESE

Electronics has replaced the "dairymaid's thumb" with a transducer to monitor the development of the rigidity of curd during the manufacture of cheese. The transducer has been used to automate an existing system resulting in improved accuracy and a reduction in labour. Previously an operator was required to adjust a micro-meter continuously and to record corresponding times. This is now done by electrical signals from the transducer which are displayed on a chart recorder. The instrument could also find applications in medicine, and in the food, oil and paint industries.

(*Financial Times 21.8.78*)

### ROBOT IN HOT POWDER FORGING OPERATION

Hot-forging via the powder metallurgy route is gaining a great deal of interest among engineering, particularly in the US and Sweden. Contrasted with conventional forging procedures, hot P/M forging permits better control of physical properties and results in a part needing less machining. But if costs cannot be kept low, these benefits soon disappear.

ESP, is using robot handling on production runs in which lot sizes run from 10,000 to 40,000. The equipment used is a Unimate industrial robot *and production labour has been roughly halved*. The decisions to go over to the robot handler was made some three years ago and it resulted in the development of what is an interlocked and synchronised production system made up of the feeder for the sintered compacted parts, the controlled atmosphere furnace, the forging presses and the robot itself.

General purpose robots of this type are programmable, parts handling or tool-handling machines able to control and synchronise the equipment with which they are working. The ESP unit has an electronic memory and control system to direct the actuator arm.

Unimate is building a machine with from two to six programmable arm and wrist movements and memory size runs from 128 to 2,048 steps – most industrial jobs need no more than 100 steps. Positioning repeatability is to 0.05 in.

*(Financial Times 10.8.78)*

LASER UNIT GIVES TOOL POSITION

The laser interferometer is able to perform remote positional measurements of, for example, machine tool cutting heads without direct mechanical connection with great accuracy.

A helium neon laser unit, connected to a control and calculator module, produces a beam which is split so that part of the light is directed at a remote mirror on the moving machine while the other strikes a fixed reflector.

The two reflected fluxes are beamed into a detection system located in the laser and motion of the mobile with respect to the fixed mirror causes sinusoidal modulation of the signal. The distance between two successive peaks corresponds to a half wavelength shift of 0.3 micron.

The detector signal is converted to impulses and a subsequent computer unit samples the accumulated value every 40 milli seconds: traversed distance is displayed after allowing for the wavelength and the air index.

Two kinds of reflection unit are available one for measuring displacement and velocity and the other to deal with angles and surface flatness. Setting up of the Metrilas M100 is not difficult because the light beams and optical components have a misalignment intolerance of plus or minus 2 mm. No complicated alignments calling for trained personnel are involved, so that a machine tool can be thoroughly checked and calibrated in very little time. To make a linear displacement measurement takes about ten minutes.

Readings are produced on a nine-digit display on the control unit or on a built-in thermal printer.

*(Financial Times 27.7.78)*

ELECTRONIC COLOUR PROCESS ADVANCES

Permitting, for the first time, individual input of colour pages for colour correction and storage – electronically – the Helio Data Processing System of Gravure Reproduction (HDP) could bring about major changes of reproduction methods in graphics communications.

An electronic sorting process allowers users to engrave all pages of one printing colour in the correct position on the cylinder, again by electronic means, using Hell Helio-Klischograph techniques.

Basic equipment consists of an HDP scanner, two magnetic disc stores, the electronic cylinder engraver and the control processor. The latter, a Sicomp 10, acts as a dialogue unit to feed in instructions and mode of operation in the form of hard copy. A display screen is used to check each move. Most of this input data would be needed only once and would thus be held on floppy disc for reference.

For the scanning process, the floppy disc provides operating data to the processor and specific operating instructions are keyed in. The HDP scanner provides simultaneous scanning in all four colours.

Complete scanned input data is stored on the discs. In the subsequent sorting, the operator provides instructions for imposition from a layout chart. Many modes of data handling are possible.

The next stage in the process is to transfer all the amended information to the second disc in correct sequence. The engraving programme can then begin. One cylinder each is engraved per colour, the engraving being matched to the printing specifications.

Hell development work means that gravure will have the ability to save time and materials and store colour separations in the computer, or maintain a colour library and call out pictures for colour engraving when they so decide.

(*Financial Times 9.8.78*)


GUIDE IN A WIRING LABYRINTH

Costs of wiring assembly, inspection and testing operations may be cut by as much as 50 per cent using a micro-processor-controlled wiring aid operable by semi-skilled staff.

The unit is suitable for use on any wiring assembly where the majority of wires terminate at multi-way connectors, and it relies on a patented proximity method to identify individual wires. It accelerates wiring work, makes it more accurate and can help beginners to produce perfect work.

Every wire is positively identified without stripping or tagging, prior to connection. Every connection is tested for continuity and shorts and all operations performed in the right sequence.

Included in the equipment is a data unit which can be used to create and edit wiring and testing instructions. This commands a control unit which automatically reads the information recorded on the data unit cassette. Instructions are provided on a video screen and a hand-held probe identifies, locates and tests the wires.

In operation, an instruction on the screen could tell the user to select a wiring harness and connect it to the equipment (called Thesus). The second instruction could be to locate wire No. 1 and connect it to a given point. As the probe nears the required wire an audible signal increases in volume.

Once the connection is made the probe is touched in the connection point and Thesus checks for continuity. Wiring faults would be shown on the screen and only when these have been corrected would the next instruction be displayed.

(*Financial Times 8.9.78*)

*Maintenance*

A machine tool manufacturer has tackled the problem of service engineers having to repair equipment which rarely goes wrong. They have introduced a remote diagnostic service operated over telephone lines from a fully equipped central base at its headquarters. Using equipment and a technique known as NEAT, experienced service men at headquarters can use the customer's control equipment cathode ray tube display as a "shop talk" communication device to augment voice contact by telephone, and can guide the user's maintenance man through the most comprehensive diagnostic procedures.

(*Financial Times 24.8.78*)

# 10 The structure of the electronics industry

## Labour Research Department

There can be no doubt that the electronics industry is growing. The increasing number of existing products to which electronic components are now being added as well as the widespread distribution of products which have originated from the electronics industry both testify to an explosive growth. Unfortunately is is very difficult to find world wide figures to document the increasing importance of the electronics industry. As the EEC Commission stated in its investigation into one aspect of the industry, data processing:

> "where information existed it was collected and classified in different ways from one country to another so that the compilation of data on identical bases would have involved work out of all proportion to the working party's facilities"

in addition

> "the data from studies of various origins in the Commission's possession often differed very greatly if indeed they were comparable."

> (Report concerning the developments in the data-processing sector in the Community in relation to the world situation; October 1976)

However some statistics are available. At the level of the whole industry the journal 'Electronics' estimated that in dollar terms the electronic equipment industry has grown 14 per cent between 1975 and 1977 in the US, Western Europe and Japan (World Electronic Markets. January 1977). This is well ahead of the increase in US prices of machinery and equipment which rose by about 6 per cent in both years. The figures thus represent a considerable real increase, although because of the issues examined in Chapter 9 this growth is not reflected in employment. Looking at some of the individual sectors the picture is similar. In telecommunications (which is not yet an entirely electronic industry) the number of telephones increased world-wide by 6.7 per cent each year for the ten years 1967 to 1976 (Siemens International Telephone Statistics). In data processing information collected by the US company Data General suggests that in the ten years to 1975 world sales in dollars of general purpose computer systems grew by 128 per cent. For integrated circuits the growth has been even more explosive. According to West German figures published by the EEC the world market rose from $130 million in 1965 to $1,670 million in 1973 a thirteen fold increase (Electronic Components Programme of the Federal Republic).

It would be possible to provide further statistics for other sectors of the electronics industry, for example for consumer electronics, for avionics, which represent as much as one third of value of a modern aircraft, and for electronics used in defence. However, this report is concerned only with three sectors: telecommunications, computers and integrated circuits. For each there is an outline of some of the major recent developments and the position in the UK is briefly examined. Finally a table lists the major firms in these industries giving details of sales, sales growth and employment.

Although each of these can be examined separately one of the most striking recent developments of all these industries is the way in which they have grown together. This is clearly true at a product level. Modern telephone exchanges are now computer controlled and use digital switching and transmission. Advances in computer technology depend in large measure on developments in the components supplying industry, the manufacture of integrated circuits. Microprocessors, one type of integrated circuit, are now to perform some of the functions previously carried out by large main-frame computers. Convergence is also happening at company level. International Business Machines (IBM) has developed its own private telephone exchange and although it does not sell integrated circuits (ICs) it is one of the world's largest IC manufacturers. National Semiconductors, best known as an IC company has expanded into point of sale equipment with its Datachecker and now competes with long established companies in this field.

As well as companies which have extended their main area of interests into other fields there are also companies which are active throughout the electronics industry. Siemens makes telecommunications equipment and computers, although its IC interests do not match the US semiconductor companies. Philips has signalled with its purchase of the US company Signetics that it intends to strengthen its presence in IC manufacturing and is a powerful competitor in world telecommunications markets. Since the collapse of Unidata, when it sold its large computer interests to Siemens it has not made large computers. The Japanese companies Fujitsu and Nippon Electric Company are both involved in computers and tele-communications and together with Hitachi and the Mitsubishi Electric Corporation are engaged in a massive IC research effort.

## Telecommunications

In telecommunications, the major recent development has been the introduction of computer controlled, stored programme control (SPC) exchanges. The advantages of an exchange of this sort are described in the Carter report on the UK Post Office:

> "Reduction of maintenance by a half, doubling of manpower productivity through centralised maintenance, reductions of installation cost and time, dramatic reductions in capital cost, improvements in traffic measurement and management information, and better accessibility and accuracy of billing information . . . To all these benefits may be added the ability to introduce a new range of services to the customer as well as increasing the reliability of existing services."
> (Report of the Post Office Review Committee, Chairman C F Carter FBA; Cmnd 6850 July 1977)

All large new telecommunications contracts have specified SPC exchanges. However it should not be forgotten that, because of existing customers, telecommunications manufacturers still have to produce electromechanical equipment. Thus, despite the move to semi-electronic exchanges taking place in the UK at present and the planned unveiling of the fully electronic System X in 1979 the Post Office is still ordering electromechanical exchange equipment. Indeed according to the Post Office's 1976 plans 24 per cent of all 1979-80 orders are to be for Crossbar and Strowger equipment. (Post Office Orders for Telecommunications Switching Equipment Report by M V Posner May 1977). Even the Swedish company L M Ericsson reported that "slightly more than half the bookings for local and trunk exchanges in 1977 were for Crossbar systems" (some of which were modernised with computer controlled registers (Annual Report)).

However, although a good deal of electro-mechanical equipment is still being produced it is the massive SPC exchange projects which have taken the headlines. The Middle East has been a major market with Saudi Arabia placing a £1,700 million order for the modernisation of its telephone network with a consortium of L M Ericsson, Philips and Bell Canada; and Egypt is set to order £1,650 million of equipment from a US consortium. With Iran and Kuwait both planning to extend and modernise their telecommunications networks the Middle East is likely to remain a major growth area. US, Western·European and Japanese companies have all tendered and been successful in the Middle East and other markets but UK companies have only been involved in a very limited way in the provision of exchanges. The reason is that they have no SPC exchange to offer. One significant company development was the decision in April 1976 of the US company Western Electric to compete for export orders outside the US. Western Electric is the manufacturing arm of American Telephone and

Telegraph (AT & T) and had previously confined itself to the massive US market (155 million telephones – 40% of the world total). Apart from the size of the company – its 1977 sales were £4,660 million – Western Electric has the most experience with SPC exchanges. It introduced its first, the ESS1 in 1965 and the most recent the ESS4 was put into service in 1976. It will be a formidable competitor for the future.

## Computers

In contrast to telecommunications the world computer market has always been dominated by the largest US company, IBM. A report by the West German government quoted by the EEC commission gave IBM a 56.6 per cent share of the world general purpose computer park at the start of 1975. No other company managed to get into double figures. (The details are in Table 1).

Table 1

*World's general purpose computer park divided by the principal manufacturers 1.1.1975.*

| Manufacturer | Park share in per cent |
| --- | --- |
| IBM | 56.6 |
| Honeywell | 8.2 |
| Univac (Sperry) | 6.5 |
| Manufacturers of COMECON | 5.2 |
| Japanese manufacturers | 4.7 |
| Burroughs | 4.6 |
| I.C.L. | 3.1 |
| Unidata* | 2.7 |
| NCR | 2.4 |
| Others | 6.0 |
| Total | 100.0 |

*Split up in 1975

(Third data processing programme of the Federal Government (West Germany 1976-79)).

IBM's current sales continue to reflect its strong position. Thus according to figures published in IDC's European Market Report IBM has a 54.5 per cent market share by value in Western Europe in 1977. This is almost exactly the same as the 1974 figure of 54.0 per cent. However, there are two developments which indicate that IBM's dominance in the market may be under threat in the long term. The first is the emergence of the Japanese and their associates in the US; the second is changes in the nature of the computer industry itself.

The West German study puts the Japanese share of the world computer park at only 4.7 per cent in 1975. But this figure represents the results of previous years of sales and since that date the growth of the Japanese industry has been rapid. Thus from 1974 to 1977 sales of the telecommunications and computer company Fujitsu rose from £174 million to £701 million (at current exchange rates) a four fold increase. The sales of the Nippon Electric Company also increased from £271 million to a figure almost four times higher, £1,039 million, in the same period. This growth is more than twice as fast as IBM's growth in sales which rose from £5,417 million in 1974 to £10,388 million in 1977. IBM's sales were still 10 times the sales of NEC in 1977 but more significantly in 1974 they had been 20 times larger.

The growing strength of the Japanese companies is not surprising given that Japan is the second largest market for data processing equipment and given also the vast Japanese research and development effort (see section on integrated circuits). It is complemented by the sales efforts of the US companies Amdahl and Itel which are technically linked with the Japanese companies Fujitsu and Hitachi and which have taken sales from IBM by providing machines which are entirely compatible with existing IBM hardware and programs. (The Japanese Ministry for International Trade and Technology has organised Fujitsu, Hitachi and Mitsubishi into a grouping, the Computer Development Laboratory, to develop IBM compatible computers).

The second threat to the dominance of IBM is the shift away from large and medium mainframe computers to minis and micros. This will probably not result in an absolute decline in mainframe sales but current forecasts are that sales of smaller computers will grow more rapidly. Thus the EEC Commission report quoted the following sale forecasts for the EEC in the period 1974 to 1979: central processors and systems – increase annually by 10.5 per cent; micro computers – increase annually by 17 per cent (Sobemap Study). Information available at company level confirms the more rapid growth at the smaller end of the market. In the period 1974 to 1977 IBM's sales figures rose from £5,417 million to £10,388 million a 92 per cent increase (current exchange rates). The sales of Data General Corporation and Digital Equipment Corporation, the two companies making small computers grew considerably more rapidly. For Data General the increase was from £35 million to £146 million up 310 per cent; for Digital Equipment Corporation (DEC) sales rose from £180 million in 1974 to £607 million in 1976 – a 227 per cent increase.

As the EEC study pointed out:

"unlike large scale data processing, no marked denomination of one firm can be found in the peri-informatic sub-sector taken as a whole."

(Peri-informatic is the word coined by the Commission to cover mini and micro computers, peripherals, interactive equipment and data acquisition equipment.)

IBM does not dominate this sector as it does the manufacture of mainframe computers, although it has a very successful mini-computer, the Series 1.

Future developments in this area are impossible to predict. The growing move to dispersed data processing (micro computers widely distributed throughout the system, for example in industrial process control) removes some of the functions of a large mainframe computer. But is also increases the amount of information available to the mainframe computer which it can itself analyse. In company terms the development of microprocessors and the convergence between IC producers and computer manufacturers is likely to bring more IC manufacturers into the micro computer market.

**Integrated circuits**

Integrated circuits are the most rapidly growing section of the electronic industry. As with computers the industry is dominated by US manufacturers although no single company is predominant in ICs. The major US companies are Texas Instruments, the Fairchild Camera and Instrument Corporation, Motorola, National Semiconductor, Intel and Mostek. The Japanese are making great efforts to increase the size of their industry with a consortium of the largest electronic companies carrying out joint research. Major Western European companies also make ICs and the IC operations of ITT should be added to these because all its IC manufacturing is in Europe.

However, it is very important to distinguish two strands in IC production. One is the manufacture of multi-application integrated circuits, which are made in massive volumes and are standard throughout the world. The other is the production of ICs for a particular purpose, where only a small number are made. There is range of production levels between these two extremes but the distinction between the two is important because the manufacture of multi-application world standard chips and custom designed ICs for the specialist market are virtually two separate industries.

It is multi-application ICs that competition is fiercest and where the US companies' dominance is clearest. Apart from Philips the manufacture of multi-application ICs in Western Europe is at present confined to the subsidiaries of US companies (including ITT). The lack of these products is unfortunate as it is in the development of new products for high volume manufacture that production technology is most advanced. This was recognised by the UK Sector Working Party on the industry when it stated:

"The technology and experience of volume production of selected (multi-application) circuits will increasingly be needed to help to develop the technology required for many of the custom circuits in the future."

(The Microelectronics Industry June 1978)

The Japanese effort is concentrated on multi-application products and its total spending on their development is likely to be £550 million in the four years 1976 to 1979. The need to move into multi-application products appears also to have been recognised in Western Europe with the creation of Inmos and GEC's planned link with Fairchild as well as a possible tie up between Motorola and the French company Thomson CSF.

Although the past has seen the rapid growth of companies on the back of new technological advances for example Intel with first the 4004 microprocessor and then the 8080 this may occur less frequently in the future. Research costs are very high. For example the Chairman of Texas Instruments has stated that his company alone will match Japanese research and development expenditure between 1977 and 1979. (One fruit of the Texas Instruments research programme very recently announced was the start of volume production of a 64,000 cell memory (64K RAM). Fujitsu has already produced one design but it requires two separate voltages. The Texas Instruments memory cell operates on a single voltage.)

### The situation in the UK

In telecommunications the British industry, General Electric Company (GEC), Plessey and STC (a subsidiary of ITT) is effectively unable to compete in world markets for exchanges because it cannot offer an SPC exchange. Its total share of world trade in telecommunications equipment had fallen from 25 per cent in 1963 to 5.9 per cent in 1975. This situation will continue until the introduction of System X (to go on show in Geneva in October 1979). System X provides stored programme and digital switching and transmission and the UK industry is the only one outside North America to be taking these two steps simultaneously. However, this risk must now be taken; System X is in the words of the Carter report "a make or break project for the United Kingdom." Without success for System X it is hard to see how telecommunications manufacture at least for export, could continue in the UK.

In computers the mainframe industry in the UK comprises ICL and the UK manufacturing subsidiaries of IBM and other US companies whose operations are determined outside the UK. In addition GEC and Ferranti have very limited interests in mini computers (with a high dependence on the military market) and the small Computer Technology Ltd (400 employees) makes mini computers. ICL's sales have grown at about the same speed as those of IBM in the period 1974 to 1977 (current exchange rates) but are only one twentyfifth the size of those of the US company. In the UK in the period 1974 to 1977 ICL's market share has remained constant at about 27 per cent of the total market. ICL's interest in the growing area of mini computers is limited to the machines which came to it on the purchase of Singer's computer interests.

In contrast with the static picture presented by the UK computer industry, the semiconductor industry is undergoing a number of major developments. At present it consists of subsidiaries of six US companies, one Dutch company and three UK companies, but the products they make are very different. The subsidiaries of Texas Instruments, Motorola and National Semiconductors make world standard ICs in the UK. But their production here does not include the technically most advanced products. The subsidiaries of General Instruments and Hughes Micro electronics concentrate on custom ICs for the specialist market. And the three UK owned companies Ferranti, GEC and Plessey operate in a similar way. Only the UK subsidiaries of Philips and ITT are involved in the development of advanced multi-application ICs.

However this is about to change. The NEB has set up a new company, Inmos, to make microprocessors and 64,000 cell memories. Initially research and development will be undertaken in the USA where some 1,000 jobs will be created but in time production in the UK is to employ 4,000. GEC has announced a joint venture with Fairchild to produce microprocessors and the 16K RAM in the UK. Some 1,000 jobs are expected to be created. Both these projects contain the danger that the most technically advanced work remains in the US – with the 1,000 US workers in the Inmos venture and with Fairchild in the GEC-Fairchild link-up. However they are important steps along the road towards the development and production of the most technologically advanced ICs in the UK.

Table 2

*Major electronic companies (telecommunications, computers and integrated circuits)\**

| | | Sales in 1977† £m | Increase on 1974† % | Employees (000) |
|---|---|---|---|---|
| IBM (US) | Computers | 10,388 | +92 | 310 |
| ITT (US) | Telecommunications & Others (a) | 7,530 | +58 | 375 |
| Philips (Netherlands) | Electricals | 7,280 | +73 | 392 |
| Siemens (West Germany) | Electricals | 6,220 | +118 | 319 |
| Western Electric (US) | Telecommunications | 4,660 | +48 | 162 |
| Rockwell (US) | Electronics & aerospace (b) | 3,360 | +78 | 115 |
| Hitachi (Japan) | Electricals | 2,770 | +222 | 73 |
| GTE (US) | Telecommunications (c) | 2,360 | +5 | 203 |
| GEC (UK) | Electricals | 2,340 | +66 | 191 |
| CGE (France) | Electricals | 2,210 | +81 | 170 |
| Sperry Rand (US) | Electronics & aerospace | 1,870 | +68 | 86 |
| Honeywell (US) | Automation equipment | 1,670 | +74 | 76 |
| Mitsubishi Electric (Japan) | Electricals | 1,490 | +213 | 52 |
| NCR (US) | Business systems | 1,440 | +70 | 67 |
| Burroughs (US) | Data processing | 1,220 | +86 | 51 |
| Texas Instruments (US) | Semi conductors & electronics | 1,170 | +74 | 69 |
| NEC (Japan) | Telecommunications | 1,040 | +283 | 32 |
| Ericsson (Sweden) | Telecommunications | 960 | +54 | 66 |
| CDC (US) | Computers | 870 | +84 | 46 |
| Motorola (US) | Semi conductors & other products | 830 | (+51)†† | 56 |
| Fujitsu (Japan) | Computers | 700 | +303 | 33 |
| Northern Telecom (Canada) | Telecommunications | 680 | +61 | 25 |
| Thomson CSF (France) | Electronics | 660 | +111 | 52 |
| Plessey (UK) | Telecommunications & electronics | 610 | +53 | 59 |
| DEC (US) | Small computers | 610 | +227 | 36 |
| ICL (UK) | Computers | 420 | +108 | 32 |
| Fairchild (US) | Integrated circuits | 260 | +60 | 20 |
| National Semi conductors (US) | Integrated circuits | 220 | +143 | 22 |
| Intel (US) | Integrated circuits | 160 | +181 | 8 |
| Ferranti (UK) | Electronics | 160 | +82 | 17 |
| Data General (US) | Small computers | 150 | +310 | 9 |

*Many of the companies in this table manufacture products other than telecommunications, computers and integrated circuits. The table may be of some use in giving sales, employee and growth figures for the major companies involved in electronics. It should also be remembered that because the figures are in pounds sterling much of the percentage growth shown is a result of price increases.

†Sales for year ending in 1977 with the exception of Ferranti, Plessey and GEC which are for years ending in March 1978.The comparative sales figures have also been brought forward by one year.

††Latest figure 1976

(a) Telecommunications accounted for 23 per cent of sales in 1977.
(b) Electronics accounted for 19 per cent of sales in 1977.
(c) Includes operation of telecommunications. Manufacturing accounted for 45 per cent of sales.

# 11 Computer aided administration

### Peter Hansen,
### The National Computing Centre

*"It is unworthy of excellent men to lose hours like slaves in the labour of calculation" - Gottfried von Leibniz, 1646-1716.*

Von Leibniz made this observation some 300 years ago to justify the invention of his own rather primitive calculating machine. He would no doubt have approved of the thousands of pocket calculators, word processors, computer terminals and mini computers which can be found in our own offices today: and perhaps our grandchildren will look back in horror at the thousands of people who were confined in offices doing routine, repetitive manual tasks, much as we look back in horror at the enormities of the Victorian factory system.

What are we trying to achieve by office automation? Are we trying to release the "excellent men" (and women, of course) from unnecessary labour and given them more time for carrying our the more creative office jobs: the research, planning, controlling and creative writing that is the mainstay of most enterprises, but which is often neglected because of the constant stream of routine work? Or are the objectives more mundane than that? To save time and money and cut back on man-power? Like most things in life, there is never usually a grand design. Things tend to evolve. Someone invents something which seems to him like a good idea without really thinking through the full implications of that idea; someone takes it up; others follow the trend; and before we know it, a whole way of life has evolved round a single man's clever idea. One only has to think what Alexander Graham Bell started by inventing the telephone!

So it is with computers: what started off as an obscure scientific device confined to calculations in research laboratories, has evolved into a device, which eventually may sit, as familiar an object as the telephone, in every office and household in the land. Like the telephone, they are and will be, a great convenience, a labour-saving device; but also, in times of stress, they will probably get blamed, like the telephone, for a great deal of what is wrong with the office system; and in time, the original objectives for which the machine was installed may be forgotten.

The Department of Employment conducted a survey of computers in offices in the mid-sixties and then again in the early seventies*, in which organisations were asked why they had installed a computer. In the earlier survey the principal reply was "to reduce costs." In the second survey the principal reply was "to provide a better service to management." Cynics might observe that in the intervening years organisations had discovered that they hadn't saved any money by introducing computers and had settled for a less quantifiable reason. With the benefit of hindsight however, it is sensible to suggest that the second reply is the answer they should have given originally: anyone introducing a computer merely to reduce costs has obviously not given the project sufficient thought. The true reason for introducing a computer should be whether it is going to benefit the enterprise not only economically, but socially and technically as well. Is it going to make the output more accurate, or the technical content better, and are people going to enjoy doing the work more with computers than without them?

Before we can answer these questions we ought perhaps to consider in a little more detail just what work it is that computers are taking over in the office and how these trends are likely to develop.

First of all, routine clerical work such as calculation, typing, filing and so on. This is the area in which computers have probably made the most impact so far. From the earliest days it became obvious that the computer was going to be good at large-scale, regular tasks such as invoicing and payroll. Originally only the very largest organisations could justify using computers for these tasks; but as computers have got smaller and cheaper then many more organisations have installed them for these jobs. The armies of typists and clerks gave way to armies of girls punching cards and clerks checking the results. There was very little redundancy, but a lot of re-training took place. Now the typists are more likely to be found keying information directly into the computer via a terminal; and much of the checking has been programmed into the computer itself; so that some clerical checking jobs have disappeared, but redundancy is still not causing a problem. Indeed, I have heard on Trade Union official remark that far from considering computers a threat, they have usually welcomed their introduction, as they seem to have created far more work than they have eliminated! Although this remark was made tongue in cheek, there is certainly more than an element of truth in it. Computers should be helping to stimulate the growth and productivity; and this growth should in the long term create more work; I don't think this was what my Trade Union friend had in mind, however!

---

*"Computers in Offices 1972" HMSO.

If redundancy is not a threat, then what about the question of social acceptability? Is work with computers more enjoyable than manual clerical work, or less? The National Computing Centre recently conducted a survey on the effects of computers on people's work, and found some contradictory answers. In one organisation where girls had produced invoices manually, and had a considerable amount of typing and calculation to do, the operation had been computerised to the extent where they merely keyed the item numbers and quantities into the computer, and the computer did the rest. Some of the girls welcomed the change because they felt their jobs were now a lot easier; others felt the work was less demanding and consequently more boring. In this case the computer had unintentionally sorted the sheep from the goats; and if there were to be a happy ending to the story it would surely be to leave the contented ones at it; and find more demanding work for those whose aptitude was no longer being satisfied; and who obviously had the skill to do more than routine clerical work.

At one time, only those clerical jobs with a calculation element in them were affected by computers; but with the advent of the word processor this has changed. The word processor can best be described as a computerised typewriter. Standard letters, reports, price lists, brochures and other things which need frequent typing and updating are typed on a fairly conventional typewriter, but initially no paper is produced; only a line image appears on a television screen above the typewriter. Corrections can be made to the image before the typescript is committed to hard copy. A copy is simultaneously being built up on to a tape cassette or diskette, which can be used for subsequent amendment and reproduction. Insert the cassette into the typewriter and key in the required number of copies, and they are rattled off at high speed. If at any time changes are needed, then the typist can access the appropriate page and line on the cassette and make the necessary change to the master copy on tape. Even insertions can be made without affecting the rest of the copy.

Another clerical job affected by computers is that of the filing clerk. Computers have held records on magnetic tape or disc for many years, but many organisations need to have a legible copy of many records quickly available, so that the paperwork problem of filing these records has remained with them. Now however, computers are able to output copies of records direct on to microfilm, thus reducing the record storage problem by 90%, a considerable saving in these days of soaring office rental costs. The clerical work of filing and retrieving remains, but this is nothing like the physical problem it was. So much for the clerks and typists; what of the managers, how are they affected, and how are they likely to be affected by computers?

One of the benefits usually listed when justifying the introduction of a computer is "to provide better management information," but what information can the manager expect from his computer? At one time any computer listing could be sanctified by the title "management information" and placed reverently on the manager's desk, where he was left to wrestle with it as best he could. Usually, because he wasn't sure what he was looking for or how to find it, it became dusty with neglect; until a month later a new computer listing appeared, and so on.

This problem was usually brought about and perpetuated by a lack of understanding. The manager wasn't sure what the computer could give him; the computer man wasn't sure what the manager wanted; so to make sure he couldn't be accused of inadequacy, the computer man proceeded to give the manager absolutely everything; which, of course, was too much.

Some managers have now got the message that the computer is just a big filing system; and just as you would ask your secretary to go to the filing cabinet and prepare a listing of, say, all those people who owe you more than £1000, you can get the computer people to do the same thing from the computer's files. The result is not a huge listing of everybody who owes you anything, but hopefully, a nice neat little legible report. Once the manager knows the contents of the computer's files, with the connivance of the computer people, he can manipulate any shape and size of report that he chooses; remembering of course that computer time could be costing him £100 per hour. In fact, those long meaningless listings probably cost more than the shorter, more relevant reports. It was predicted some years ago, that by the 1980s every manager would have a computer display screen on his desk, which would bring him up-to-the-minute information at the press of a button. We have certainly reached the stage where it is technically possible for every office to have a terminal hooked up to the computer; but whether it is the manager's job to waste his time pressing the buttons and communicating with the computer is another question. There still seems to be a clerical job to mediate between the manager and the machine; just as he has a secretary to sort out the routine 'phone calls and callers from the really urgent ones.

In the USA with the push-button telephone system, every telephone becomes a potential computer terminal. Many computers are now able to give a voice response; so we are getting very near the day when the computer is only a 'phone call away from providing us with the information we require.

Another device which has greatly improved the quality of management information is the graphics terminal. Here we can have displayed on a television screen, graphs, bar charts and the like in full colour.

In the area of control, the manager has an increasingly useful tool in the computer. Credit control, and similar financial controls, can be catered for by well-constructed management reports from the computer's files. Budgetary control, for instance, is merely a question of feeding in all the organisation's income and expenditure under various headings, getting the computer to compare these with pre-set targets, and warning management of any over – or under – achievement.

A more sophisticated approach to long term planning is to use the computer for financial modelling, or perhaps creating a marketing model. Here the computer tries to answer the question "What would happen if . . .?" The manager can feed in various prices and market constraints, and the computer tries to simulate the effect of these on sales or future company growth. Needless to say, the computer is never going to be able to predict the future accurately, any more than a crystal ball; but the manager has the satisfaction of knowing that with all the facts available and the computer's powers of calculation he has made the most scientific guess possible.

At the smaller end of the market, it is possible to buy a fully program-mable microcomputer, with memory, video-display and print-out for under £1000: a device which has as much power as a whole roomful of equipment costing 100 times as much had 20 years ago.

As in other fields of electronics, power-for-pound costs are reducing yearly. It is becoming increasingly more difficult for the smaller firm not to justify a computer for some application or other; particularly as the availability of packaged programs to go on them is increasing; which means that the user does not have to recruit expensive specialist staff to write programs for him.

We have entered the era of the electronic office. Will we yet see the paperless office? This depends on the reaction of the general public. Are you ready to accept a reminder about your unpaid telephone bill on the kitchen display screen; warning you that you will automatically be cut off by the computer unless you key in a debit to your bank account on your terminal immediately? Or would you still prefer the red statement coming through the letter box?

That office staff can and should be released for more productive work is another point that needs careful consideration.

In 1953 the proportion of administrative, technical and clerical workers in manufacturing industry was 18.2% of the total employees. In 1971 this had risen to 27.4%*. In other words in 1953 four out of five workers were producing goods; in 1971 the ratio was only three out of four. If the computer can set the trend in the opposite direction, it can surely do nothing but good for the prosperity of the country as a whole.

---

*"Computers in Offices 1972" HMSO.

# 12

# Computer aided design An appraisal of the present state of the art

## Computer Aided Design Centre

### Introduction

This section describes the area of influence of Computer Aided Design and Manufacture and explains why the subject is receiving increased attention throughout industry.

### 1.1 *Over-all context*

COMPUTER AIDED DESIGN (CAD) is the application of systematic procedures and computing devices to the function of product design. COMPUTER AIDED MANUFACTURE (CAM) is the use of similar technique in Manufacturing, Planning and Production Scheduling.

The over-all context of CAD and CAM is shown diagrammatically in Figure 1 where its major area of influence on the manufacturing process is illustrated. It can be seen that CAD and CAM occupy a key position in the over-all system and, as industrial progress proceeds, the automation of these activities is emerging as a major contribution to increased industrial productivity.

Progress in the exploitation of computers for design and manufacture is being accelerated by a number of factors. Among these are the increased use of mathematical techniques in the design process and the increasing use of automatic machines in the manufacturing process. Both of these developments increase the use of numerical data which is an essential prerequisite for the effective deployment of computers.

Independent of advances in industrial design technologies and manufacturing processes, computer and computer-software technologies have developed in such a way that their versatility is vastly increased and costs are lowered. The basic attributes of computers remain the same, i.e. their ability to undertake complex calculations and their speed of handling large volumes of data accurately. These have been considerably enhanced, however, by techniques in data communication, data-storage technology

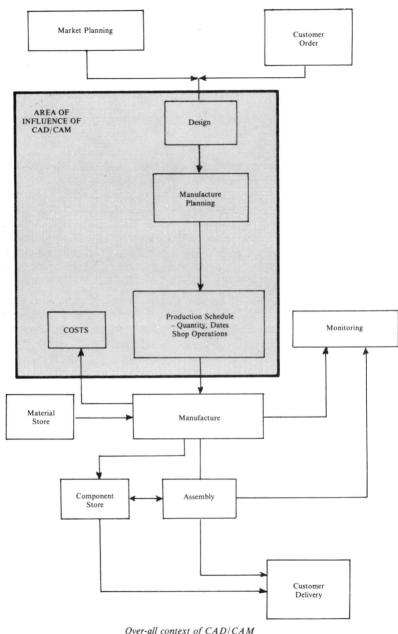

*Over-all context of CAD/CAM*
Figure 1

and developments at the man/machine interface, i.e. interactive graphics. Whereas advances in data communication and data storage have given the impetus to bridging the gap between CAD and CAM, it is the advances in computer graphics which have encouraged the use of computers in the design field. Progress is taking place, therefore, on several fronts simultaneously.

## 1.2 *Computer aided design*

The benefits arising from using a computer as an aid to design stems from the inherent complexity of establishing a 'best' design. It is seldom possible to determine the best design solely by mathematical calculation, because the most satisfactory design is usually a compromise between functional, aesthetic and manufacturing considerations. Judgement on what is 'best', therefore, depends upon the calculated forecast of performance, external appearance and suitability of the design for manufacture. The first of these considerations involves mathematical calculations, the second a judgement on probable appearance and the third on an examination of the economics of production. Some factors are quantifiable, others are not, and the interactions between the various elements are beyond the scope of normal mathematical procedures.

The design process, therefore, requires a high degree of human involvement to initiate ideas and to progress design from development to its final stage. Thus, even in a computer-driven design system, the computer assists (but does not supplant) the designer, who continues to take final responsibility. The usual method by which this co-operation between designer and computer is achieved is for the computer to undertake those calculations and data transformations which are of a routine and time-consuming nature, thus freeing the designer for the crucial decision-making duties.

Such interactive techniques are incorporated into complete systems in such a way that they are capable of operation by a minimum of directives from the designer. Often such systems are capable of producing complete working drawings or pictorial representations of the product on a Cathode Ray Tube. This 'visualisation' of products is one of the corner stones of computer aided design and is a key element in the interactive process by which the computer acts as an extension of the designer's intellect and increases his productivity.

Computer aided design processes have been deployed successfully in this way in applications as diverse as building construction, electrical circuit design, oil refinery layout and engineering component manufacture. Earlier systems produced drawings and displays in single colour but, increasingly, multi-colour representation is being used. Where use is made of multi-colour display systems, artistic judgements (as required in carpet manufacture, wall paper fabric, etc) are encompassed.

### 1.3 *Design information control*

Most engineering design offices are involved in handling very large volumes of numerical data, the extent of which is not perhaps obvious at first glance. The output of a typical drawing office is usually measured in terms of complete drawings; each drawing however, represents a definitive geometrical shape which is capable of being represented numerically. Indeed, the dimensional interactions between piece parts are a matter of major concern in any product made of parts. Numerical data and geometrical relationships are, therefore, the main units of engineering design. This fundamental concept is the basis of design systems which use computers, because the speed and accuracy of handling data are the computer's greatest attribute. In consequence, machines which capture engineering drawing information in digital form, and data storage and manipulation techniques, are essential components in such systems.

Additional complexities arise with the need for design modifications. In complex projects, designs are changed many times during the life of the product and it is essential that modifications are controlled in such a way that related parts are produced with matching characteristics. The complications which arise when many modifications have to be considered with overlapping timescales give rise to control problems for which the computer is eminently suited.

### 1.4 *Computer aided manufacture*

The over-all relationship between design, planning of manufacturing and production scheduling was illustrated in Figure 1 and it can be seen that these three activities are closely related. A more detailed examination of CAM is given in Chapter 13 which has been prepared by the National Engineering Laboratory and the following brief reference to CAM is intended as a lead-in to that paper.

Convenience (and, to some extent, convention) dictates that the design is passed to manufacture in the form of drawings. It has been noted that the entire drawing can be defined in digital form and this numerical data can be recreated automatically into line representations, where this is the required form of display.

The other important consideration is that this recorded numerical data can be transformed into coded instructions, capable of directing automatically-controlled machine tools. The best known of these devices are the numerically controlled (NC) milling machines, lathes and machining centres, but NC systems are also being increasingly deployed in wiring machines, flame cutters, spark-erosion machines and even automatic component assembly machines. One of the limitations on the effective use of these high-productivity methods, however, concerns the production of the operating instructions; to produce these manually requires a high degree of skill and sustained concentration. Errors are difficult to avoid and the cost of mistakes is high. It is not surprising, therefore, that the quest for computer aided methods is considered to be a matter of high priority in the over-all strategy of increased factory automation.

### 1.5 *Benefits of computer aided design and manufacture*

The over-all effect of using computer methods is to increase directly the productivity and effectiveness of those key stages in the design and production planning activities. Good design and automatic data flow between design and production, however, bring a number of further benefits. This is especially true where the actual production processes are themselves being improved to include an increased degree of automation. Indeed, it is not possible to obtain fully the rewards from increased factory automation unless production planning processes are improved at the same time.

It is widely recognised, however, that the determined use of CAD and CAM can bring positive benefits. Increased industrial effectiveness will be obtained because of:-

– better utilisation of scarce design skills;
– shortened production lead times;
– quicker response to requests for quotations;
– easier recognition of component interactions;
– smoothing of workload giving more efficient utilisation of facilities;
– reduction of errors between design and manufacture;
– introduction of automatic techniques leading to further improvements;
– reduction in tooling costs by use of NC techniques;
– better cost control;
– easier introduction of desirable modifications;
– better records which enable existing designs and parts to be identified and used;
– better matching of designs with available manufacturing plant;
– better over-all control because of readily available data.

## Trends in industrial sectors

### 2.1 *Electrical and electronics sector*

#### 2.1.1 MARKET TRENDS

The export market splits into two types of product:
(a) Basic systems, (e.g. telecommunications, distribution systems, military electronics), for countries wishing to build up an infrastructure themselves, i.e. Middle East, Asia, South America.

(b) Advanced systems offered to rich countries e.g. OPEC, (and possibly to EEC and North America); for example nuclear plants, defence systems, communication/TV networks and computers.

In all export areas, the trend may be for the purchasing country to provide an increasing proportion of the component elements of a contract (e.g. transformers, motors and terminals) as a way of supporting local industry. This will mean that the UK growth point will be in systems design.

The home market should develop in two areas;
(a) improving the UK infrastructure with better communications, information handling and transportation,
(b) re-equipping the UK manufacturing industry. Although components will be manufactured in the UK in order to support its industry, it is expected that the pressure of world trade will force import of components from those countries which are customers for UK system exports.

The trend in the UK towards greater emphasis on better systems design using imported components points clearly to the wider use of microcomputer/software control methods in place of electronic/mechanical mechanisms. This is already happening with the introduction of computer-controlled power transmission systems, NC machines and automated plant control, and computer-controlled telephone exchanges.

The increasing volume of manufacturing data resulting from more complex designs will put greater pressures on drawing offices. This is where the introduction of design changes or the provision of optical design features could be impeded, unless more effective procedures for improving data flow are developed and used.

### 2.1.2 ADOPTION OF CAD/CAM

The electronics area of the industry has been one of the earliest users of CAD/CAM techniques. The larger companies have been particularly active in the area of Integrated Circuit (IC) component design, circuit and logic analysis and test pattern generation to check designs. In production areas, most effort has been expended on the automatic laying out and manufacture of printed circuit boards (pcb). The larger companies have had considerable success with pcb systems but their systems are generally not suitable for use by other small firms.

In the heavy electrical area there is considerably lower acceptance of CAD/CAM techniques. Power system fault analysis systems are widely used but general control systems (process design) have proved too complex or too large to simulate. The future trend will be in the use of CAM to aid the assembly of systems by providing wiring lists, component requirements parts lists and production schedules, together with the computer aided generation of the definitive set of schematic drawings for system design.

There is, in general, adequate design manpower in the industry, but there is a lack of knowledge of CAD/CAM techniques.

## 2.2 *Mechanical engineering sector*

### 2.2.1 MARKET TRENDS

The history of mechanical engineering in the UK since the Second World War is depressing, with the continual erosion of markets by overseas competition.

It has been accepted for a long time that the solution lies in better designed products and better manufacturing methods, but progress towards this has been slow. The trend has been for Aerospace (with the most technically demanding product) to lead in design and development techniques. These have filtered down into other sectors, particularly cars, ship-building and diesel engines, usually with external encouragement, e.g. the Engineering Sciences Data Unit.

There is often a large volume of design data generated which is leading to a growing trend towards computer draughting aids. In addition, competitive manufacturing techniques need production planning and rationalisation made possible by the integration of computer aided design and manufacture and (arising from this) the need for improving the flow of design data.

### 2.2.2 ADOPTION OF CAD/CAM

The Aerospace industry has been an early user of CAD/CAM. In the design analysis area, a few general purpose (and many special-purpose) programs are widely used; e.g. stress analysis and control systems simulation of computer aided product data management and NC tape preparation are used; database systems and computer networks are in use and are being continously developed.

In automobile, ship and prime mover design, CAD is used for analysis and simulation by the larger companies using in-house mainframe computers or bureaux services, but less extensively than in aerospace. Some integration of design and manufacture has been achieved e.g. car body panels, and some companies have invested in CAD specific to their product, (e.g. David Brown with gearboxes).

Attempts have been made by universities to find applications for mechanism theory in industry (particularly textile machinery), with limited success. Several consultancies, often based in universities, offer CAD expertise as part of a problem-solving capability in mechanical engineering.

A few large companies have invested in draughting systems, but many companies recognise the limitations of 'drawing-only' systems and require better interfaces with analysis programs. Nevertheless, the market for 'pure draughting' systems is increasing.

The companies using NC machine tools cover the whole spectrum of size. Tape preparation is done manually in a large proportion of them, and the remainder use mainly packages available on time-sharing bureaux. Outside the aerospace sector, the use of in-house mainframes is rare, but the use of desk-top mini-computers is increasing.

### 2.3  Chemical engineering sector

#### 2.3.1 MARKET TRENDS

The process industries suffer from a cyclical sequence of investment boom and subsequent slump from over-capacity. Since the last slump, in 1971/2, the UK industry has been growing steadily in the manufacturing and contracting area, although the equipment suppliers have suffered from severe foreign competition. Recent predictions indicate that the UK investment in new plant will continue to rise in the foreseeable future, and steady rather than rapid growth appears to be the world trend. There is likely to be further investment in multiproduct, multicompany complexes developed around major plant for the production of important intermediates such as ethylene.

Many large companies undertake their own developments in computer aided design and deploy considerable effort in this field. Others, however, recognise the benefit of using independent sources to supplement and assist their in-house efforts. Smaller/medium companies are already shifting towards using properly supported design software, which will become increasingly adopted by the medium and small companies. This is likely to be particularly true of the equipment suppliers, where design is closely constrained by codes of practice.

The development of software aids for design, in accordance with codes of practice, will become increasingly important to the smaller companies in their fight to survive in a highly competitive market.

Design of a process plant necessitates computer techniques to produce and handle the large volumes of complex data. The interfacing of various design tasks is growing in importance to manufacturers and contractors as a means of design integration. Similarly, the concept of design integration based on a common data-base is attracting the attention of equipment suppliers. In common with Electrical and Mechanical engineering the common element is the need to improve design and manufacture by more efficient flow of data.

#### 2.3.2 ADOPTION OF CAD/CAM

The major chemicals manufacturers and contractors are large organisations and they have invested in computer aided design since the early 1950s. Initial developments were specific in nature and, although there were many failures, some were very successful, thus motivating further investment. Accordingly, most of the large companies have a library of internally created software, but increasing costs of development and maintenance are causing all but the largest companies to turn, at least in part, to specialist suppliers. The growth of US companies, Chemshare and SSI, in the process design field are indicative of this trend.

Thus, the current level of adoption of CAD by contractors, and larger manufacturers is high, particularly for certain applications such as process design, cost estimating, pipe stressing and pipe detailing.

The equipment suppliers, being of smaller size, have been slower to turn to CAD, but a few larger companies have made significant investment and usage. More recently, with the increasing accessibility of bureaux and desk-top computers, more companies have used computers for relatively simple repetitive calculations, most, however, do not have the expertise to develop the complex systems required to make significant improvement on their ability to compete successfully.

## 2.4 Construction industry sector

### 2.4.1 MARKET TRENDS

To some extent, the overseas market has been encouraged by the depressed state of the construction industry in the UK. The cyclic pattern of capital investment in the industry is largely governed by public spending because the major construction areas are government funded, e.g. roads, schools, hospitals.

The most significant trends in the industry are in the apparent moves towards rationalisation and an increase in public participation. The former is leading towards standardisation and data co-ordination, which, in common with all other engineering sectors, require efficient computer techniques to improve communication of information. Computer draughting will also play an increasingly important role in this context, being motivated by a shortage of skilled draughtsmen and by possible changes in fee structures for the design disciplines.

The latter is forcing a greater emphasis on environmental considerations, e.g. visual impact, aesthetic appeal, safety standards, energy performance of buildings. A secondary effect is the need to consider also geographical and planning information.

Many large companies undertake their own developments and will require software facilities. Others recognise the need to take independent advice. The current interest in computer draughting is likely to continue and will create increasing demand for consultancy.

In common with electrical, mechanical and chemical equipment manufacturers, those supplying the construction industry are moving towards the use of CAD/CAM (e.g. prefabricated building manufacturers).

The construction industry embraces the production of maps (surveying), and the manipulation of inherent information e.g. earthworks, excavation, drainage, etc. There is a growing trend in this area, illustrated also by the worldwide trend towards the use of computer aids by Public Utility Companies (e.g. Electricity Boards), where the map provides and maintains the basic design information.

The professional bodies are making positive plans to provide mid-career training with emphasis on the use of computers and undergraduate training is being reviewed.

### 2.4.2 ADOPTION OF CAD/CAM

Computer aids have already been developed in the design and analysis area, e.g.

★ finite element analysis
★ civil engineering
★ structural engineering

To a lesser extent:

★ architectural design
★ heating and ventilating analysis.

In some cases these developments have taken place within the large companies and, in other cases, software has been offered on a bureau basis. In almost all cases, the existing CAD/CAM programs have been directed towards specific applications (e.g. hospital design). There is a very large quantity of such programs but there has been little to benefit the great profusion of smaller companies involved in the civil engineering sector. Attempts are being made by the Department of Environment to rectify this situation and to encourage a greater use of computers in the architectural professions, environmental design, contracting and related suppliers to the Construction Industry. It is recognised also that the industry's future use of computers depends to a great extent on its ability to rationalise the communication of information between its fragmented disciplines. A few large companies are addressing themselves to these problems. The dominant interest of the industry with regard to computing has recently changed from analytical trends to a need for overcoming the shortage of skilled draughtsmen.

### Trends in computer hardware and software

A major factor influencing the rate at which CAD is taken up and exploited by Industry is the availability and performance characteristics of computer hardware and software. This section, therefore, reviews the most significant influences and developments in this area.

### 3.1 *Hardware developments*

The computer hardware scene is one of constantly changing emphasis. The most significant change, however, during the last decade has been the decreasing physical size and increasing performance of computer systems.

### 3.1.1 LARGE COMPUTERS

In 1969, when the CAD Centre was formed, the ATLAS computer on which most of its computing activities were based had 128K words of memory and 28 million words of disc storage. This computer had a multi-access operating system capable of supporting several users on-line simultaneously. In 1978, the computers on which most of its software is developed and used have, typically, 128K words of memory and 32 million words of disc storage. They too have a multi-access Operating System capable of supporting several users on-line simultaneously.

The difference lies in the cost of these systems. The ATLAS computer configuration of 1969 cost approximately £1,500,000. The cost of the minicomputer currently used at the Centre in 1978 is £70,000. When the effect of inflation is taken into account, and due allowance made for the fact that the ATLAS was capable of supporting more users simultaneously, this represents a substantial fall in the cost of computing hardware.

### 3.1.2 MINI-COMPUTERS

This fall in cost has been most dramatic in the case of the central processor and main memory. The cost reduction has been brought about chiefly because of improvements in the technique used to mass-produce circuits of increasing complexity as single components. The development of low and medium-scale integration techniques led to the emergence of mini-computers in the early 1970s. These were based typically on a 16 bit word architecture and, in the first instance, came with rather restricted software. The last year or so, however, has seen the emergence of the 32 bit mini-computer. Over the next few years, mini-computers with word lengths greater than 16 bits will become increasingly available. These are likely to become popular because they should have the effect of reducing addressing limitations, and hence increasing the size of the programs which can be run on computer systems without the programmer having to organise his own overlays.

### 3.1.3 MICRO-COMPUTERS

The recent perfection, of large scale integration techniques, in which fifty thousand to one hundred thousand electrical components can be contained within a single chip, has led to the emergence of the micro-processor and semiconductor memories at a fraction of previous costs. It has also led to a spectacular reduction in the physical size of computer processors and memory systems. The small size and low cost of these devices is causing an explosion of new application areas for computers.

There is a wide variation in the architectures of these microprocessor systems. Bit-slicing devices are now available (4 bit, 8 bit and 16 bit microprocessors). They are already used widely to provide stand-alone business systems, and certain companies are beginning to use them in stand-alone CAD systems. At present, 8 bit microprocessors are available for a cost of ca. £20 and 16 bit microprocessors for a cost of ca. £50. The next few years will see the emergence of the 32 bit microprocessor at a comparable cost. Hardware floating point units for these devices will also be produced. While CAD software frequently makes heavy demands on computer systems, the effect of these developments will be to make these devices entirely capable of containing and satisfying the processing needs of CAD software.

One effect of the development of large-scale integration techniques has been that the Semiconductor Manufacturers now sell very cheaply the components which will enable organisations to construct their own microcomputer systems. Organisations with relatively limited expertise in electronics will be able to do this, and it will require minimal capital investment. Many of the Software Service Companies in the future are likely to assemble their own microcomputer systems and to sell hardware/software combinations.

### 3.1.4 COMPUTER MEMORY DEVICES

There is a great deal of research taking place in computer memory devices, principally in the USA. Much of this research will affect both the main computer memory and random access secondary storage devices. The research is based on a large variety of different technologies: magnetic bubble, floppy disc, charge coupled devices, semiconductor, magnetic core, magneto-optical, optical, holographic, superconductive, ferroelectric, cathode ray tube, plated wire, planer film and domain tip propagation, and will result in the emergence of very high capacity random access storage of small physical size at much lower costs than at present.

Microprocessors are already being used in the controllers of memory devices, primarily at present to reduce the number of discrete components. To a limited extent, they are also being used to detect and correct error conditions. A number of companies, including ICL, are carrying out research into the practicality of producing content-addressable mass storage devices. If these devices turn out to be practical and cost-effective it should result in a considerable simplification in the software required to drive mass storage devices.

### 3.1.5 COMPUTER PERIPHERALS

In general, the cost of magnetic tape and disc systems and input/output devices such as paper tape punches and readers, card punches and readers and line-printers has not fallen as dramatically as processors and memory.

Thus, whereas peripherals accounted for 25 per cent of the cost of a typical mini-computer configuration in 1970, it is estimated they will represent 80 percent of the hardware cost in 1980*.

In the longer term, while the cost of computer secondary storage media is likely to be reduced by the emergence of devices based on new technologies, no significant price reduction can be expected in input/ output peripherals which tend to be mechanically (rather than electrically) based. As the cheap computer processors open up new application areas, however, a large market will develop for cheap, low performance input/output peripherals.

### 3.1.6 COMPUTER GRAPHICS DEVICES

Over the past ten years, there has been an explosion in the use of computer graphics devices; these include the ink plotter and more recent electrostatic plotters as well as the visual display devices.

This period has seen substantial increases in the speed, size and quality of hard copy plotters available. Because of their large number of component mechanical parts plotters are not likely to become significantly cheaper. Microprocessors, however, will be incorporated into the controllers of these plotters so that they are able to carry out many of the functions previously carried out by the graphics software in the host processor. In the near future, these functions will include vector, arc and character generation. In a slightly longer time scale, however, it will be possible to build up, in the controller, a model of the object to be viewed so that manipulation of the picture data takes place in the plotter controller rather than in the host computer. The incorporation of these functions in the plotting device will lead to a simplification in the task of the programmer writing software for any particular graphics application, since what was previously an area of considerable complexity will now be largely concealed from him.

Visual Display Graphic Units available at the present times are of two kinds. First, there are storage tubes, which can display a picture of any complexity, but which have only a limited picture-editing capability.

Secondly, there are refreshed displays in which the displayed picture can be modified easily, but which are limited in the complexity of the picture which can be displayed.

Microprocessors will be used to provide visual display units with an increased graphics capability of the kind described for plotters. Cheap, high-performance electrical components will also be used to overcome the limitations in complexity of picture which can be displayed by refreshed devices, and to provide a means of redrawing at high speed a picture on a storage tube once it has been modified.

---

*Texas Instruments, 1977, Digital Design.

There are presently a number of refreshed colour devices available. With the exception of the CAD Centre's Advanced Visual Display Unit, most of these are American. The Japanese, however, are now beginning to enter this market. The price of these devices is falling for two reasons; (a) the rise of microprocessors reduces the number of discrete components, thus simplifying construction, (b) the price of memory components is falling. As a result, these devices can be expected to become increasingly used in applications in which powerful visualisation techniques and facilities are needed.

### 3.1.7 COMPUTER TERMINALS

The last decade has seen the alphanumeric visual display unit replace the previously ubiquitous teletype as the cheapest terminal device available. These allow alphanumeric characters to be displayed on a cathode ray screen which has to be refreshed at least twenty five times per second and cost ca. £700 each. Intelligent terminals are already available in which microprocessors are used to relieve the host computer of certain tasks concerned with the input, edit and display of data. This will become an increasingly common feature of terminals in the future.

## 3.2 *Software developments*

During the last few years, the most significant development has been the increasing software facilities provided by the computer manufacturer. When the modern mini-computer emerged in the 1970s, the software supplied by the manufacturers was limited. By the mid 1970s, however, the position has changed. There are several systems available which could provide all the necessary program development facilities, i.e. a good FORTRAN compiler, disc filing system, powerful editor and multi-access on-line operating system. It is these developments which have made it possible to produce cost-effective CAD systems.

### 3.2.1 "HIGH LEVEL" AIDS

While changes in techniques of software production have not been as dramatic as the changes in computer hardware, some improvements have occurred.

Since "high level" languages (i.e. languages understood by the computer which approximate to ordinary English) became widely available, these improvements have been based primarily on better program construction and organisation and the evolution of high level aids. By developing program modules to handle particular functions, and which can carry out these functions in a variety of different applications, it has proved possible to produce software more cheaply and reliably. For example, the CAD Centre has developed a command processor which can be incorporated into programs easily and which, when provided with a definition of the language syntax, will carry out the lexical and syntactical analysis of the input data. It has developed software to enable engineering databases to be constructed and accessed. It has developed a visualisation system which enables a wide range of pictures of objects defined in two or three dimensions to be produced on a great variety of devices. All of these are tasks which previously required highly skilled programmers. Using these tools, these tasks can now be handled by relatively inexperienced programmers. This use of existing software means that systems can be produced more cheaply and reliably (since proven tested software is being used) than by writing new software for each new application.

### 3.2.2 GRAPHICS AID

Several systems have been developed to ease the problems of drawing pictures on plotters and visual display units. One of these (GINO-F) was developed by the CAD Centre and has found wide acceptance nationally. These graphics packages are used for a variety of purposes from simple drawing of graphs to the production of two-dimensional hidden surface views of three- dimensional models. They are now so commonly used that they form part of the majority of graphics applications.

As mentioned above, it is possible to incorporate microprocessors and their associated memory chips into plotters and visual display units. Many of the graphics functions which have, until now, been carried out in the main computer processor can be performed by these intelligent devices. Operations such as line interpolation, arc-generation and clipping will no longer be carried out in the host processor. This will have a considerable effect on graphics packages such as GINO-F. Careful attention will have to be paid to the division of tasks into those best carried out in the peripheral and those best carried out in the host processor. It will be necessary, also to define an adequate communications protocol between them.

### 3.2.3 DATABASE AIDS

One of the major areas of software activity over the last few years has been the development of programming aids to enable large quantities of data to be shared between a number of different programs. Thus, in an industrial application, engineering data will be shared by a variety of programs involved in all stages from design to manufacture.

The principal purpose of this database software is to simplify the task of the applications programmer. This is achieved by providing tools for the storage and access of data without being concerned with its physical location or with the intricacies of the particular storage device on which it is held. It will provide a simplified view of the data structure in which the programmer need be concerned only with the logical relationships between those sections of the data relating to his problem.

Database structures are of two main types; navigational and relational databases. The former are suited to applications in which the data is frequently being altered. The CODASYL report had a major effect on navigational databases and is the basis of many of those commercially available. Relational databases can be interrogated very quickly but are difficult to update. They are likely to prove more popular in the future since they are particularly well suited to exploit microprocessors and the content addressable memories now being developed.

Over the next few years there will be considerable activity developing software to cope with distributed databases in which the data is dispersed over a number of linked computer installations. With improvements in computer communications and the availability of cheap computer systems, this will become an increasingly common arrangement in the future.

### 3.2.4 SINGLE USER COMPUTER SYSTEMS

As the cost of computer processors and memory devices falls, there will be an increasing tendency for CAD systems to become dedicated to a single user. This not only simplifies considerably many of the software problems, but it also ensures a good response. As long as the processor and memory are shared, the response obtained by one user depends, to a large extent, on activities of the other users of the system. This variable response time is a source of irritation to the interactive user, and its removal will lead to an increase in the acceptability of CAD systems to the engineering designer.

These cheap single user systems will mean that the benefits of CAD will become available to a much wider range of engineering companies, since a greatly reduced initial capital investment will be required. By providing a means for several of these systems to share the still relatively expensive peripherals, it will be possible for companies to expand their use of these systems economically as their requirements grow.

### 3.3 *Computer communications*

As these powerful responsive CAD systems become cheaper, they will also come to be seen increasingly as engineering tools and design aids, rather than as computer systems to be kept in a carefully protected environment, surrounded by professionals in the computer field. They will become common in engineering workshops and design offices. In order to realise the full potential of these CAD devices, however, it is clear that they must be provided with communication facilities. These will be needed to provide access to those peripherals which it will neither be practicable nor economically possible to provide locally at each CAD device. Many of these CAD systems will also need to access databases containing information, such as engineering data and company standards. These databases will be so large as to make it expensive and inconvenient to mount all this information locally. The data may also be subject to continual amendment, which will be difficult to organise if the data is held at a great number of sites. The most satisfactory solution will be to mount the database centrally so as to use communication links to access it from CAD devices. In future, provision of good communications facilities will, therefore, become very important.

While many of these functions can be carried out within one manufacturer's range of equipment, a great deal of software expertise and ingenuity is needed if the equipment comes from a number of different manufacturers. In future, there will be increasing pressure from the users of computing systems for the development and acceptance of communications standards to enable the full benefits to be gained.

An increasingly common feature over the next years will be the establishment of a number of national and international computer networks which will enable organisations to transmit data between remote sites at high speed. A number of these already exists e.g. the ARPA and EIN networks. The Post Office is itself involved in experiments such as the Experimental Packet Switching System in order to develop ways in which computer communications can be improved. The CAD Centre is playing a prominent role in this experiment. When these developments come to fruition and a high-performance, reasonably prices, national network becomes available, a major increase in computer communications can be expected from those companies which are geographically dispersed but which are not large enough to justify their own individual networks.

# 13 Computer aided manufacture in batch production

R M Sim,
National Engineering Laboratory

## Introduction

Computers are used in many parts of manufacture – wages, stock control, order processing, design, but this paper concentrates on their use in and control of metal-cutting and in particular batch manufacture.

## Batch Manufacture in Engineering

The engineering industry in the UK (Standard Industrial Classification orders VII to XII inclusive) makes a significant contribution to the GNP (about 13 per cent or £12,000m in 1974) and represents some 45 per cent of all manufacturing industry in terms of net output. It is estimated that 40 per cent of the production from the engineering industry (or £5,000m in 1974) is work produced in batches of 50 or less. In the USA it has been estimated that, by value, between 50 and 75 per cent of metal working is by batch production methods. The size of individual manufacturing units in the industry range from 17 000 units with under 100 employees (a total of 550 000 employees) producing 15 per cent of the sector, through 3 500 units with between 100 and 999 employees (a total of 1 300 000 employees) producing 35 per cent of the output, to 600 units with over 1 000 employees (a total of 1 400 000 employees) producing 50 per cent of the output.

Potential savings in the small-batch area are large both in terms of product costs and lead times. Estimates have been made that the cost of manufacturing an article in a small-batch is between 10 and 100 times larger than the cost of manufacture in mass production. This is due largely to three factors: the low capital investment in equipment for small-batch production (mainly general purpose machines); the very low utilization of these machines (10-20 per cent being typical) and the high inventory of partly finished work in small-batch production combined with the associated long lead times.

Typically, in many machine shops a batch of parts will be scheduled to undergo one operation per week. Six operations could take 6 weeks and during that time the parts will be on machine tools for only a few hours. Of these few hours less than 30 per cent on average will be productive (ie chip making). The overall picture is one of low utilization of machines and high inventory of parts due to the difficulties of organizing a variable mix of work.

### Evolution of computer aided manufacture

Prior to the advent of NC machines in the fifties, the feasible alternatives in the manufacture of components in the mid-variety, mid-volume range were transfer lines, special machinery and standard machine tools. Choice was determined by the levels of volume and variety. High volume and low variety suited transfer lines and special machinery. Low volume and high variety dictated a machine shop with a broad mixture of standard machine tools (ie a jobbing shop). NC machines introduced a further choice at the low-volume, high-variety end of the spectrum and by the mid 1970s were attracting some 10 per cent of the sales of machines in the UK. They offered significant potential improvements in productivity over conventional machines but unfortunately these improvements were not always realised – a failure to treat NC machines as components of a modern manufacturing system requiring support in a number of areas was (and still is) frequently a contributing factor.

NC is now well established in all industrialized countries and sizable supply industries are also growing in the third world – India, Taiwan, Israel and Korea. In the UK over one per cent of machine tools by number and 10 per cent by value are numerically controlled. Computers are used widely to help prepare control tapes for parts in advance of manufacture, either using languages such as APT or COMPACT, or through graphical devices used at the design stage.

By the early seventies, commercial mini-computers were being used instead of hard-wired logic in many of the control systems of NC machines. This development, known as CNC was of major benefit to the machine tool builders but also provided many useful user features – control tape storage and editing, diagnostic and monitoring capability, axis calibration and error correction and special cycle sequences. Lately microprocessors have been used increasingly in place of mini-computers. CNC systems now dominate the market. Together with the growth in microprocessor control systems there has been a gradual reduction in cost. Today the control system represents some 20 per cent of the total cost of an NC machine. Typically for a three axes machining centre costing some £100,000, the control system would cost £20,000.

By the late sixties, the concept of linking a number of NC machine tools together by control of a computer was being accepted in a few advanced companies abroad and became known as DNC. At about the same time it was realised that by adding automatic workpiece transportation to a group of DNC machines, a system could be developed which would combine the flexibility of the NC machine with some of the high productivity and lower costs of transfer lines and special machinery. This became known as FMS (flexible manufacturing system). In the States, Cook estimated cost reductions of up to 90 per cent when comparing FMS with standard machines but there is no doubt that early systems were justified solely in strictly economic terms. Systems were introduced in times of expansion of business in the companies and at least in some cases a major argument in favour of FMS was the flexibility of its manufacturing capacity (its capacity could be expanded or contracted quickly by adding or subtracting machining units or by modifying shift working). This allowed a closer match between the eventual market requirements and the production capacity of the system.

In the UK, Molins Ltd with System 24, were early leaders in the development of flexible systems for small-batch production. By 1968, a partial system had been built at their plant at Deptford and a further system was eventually installed in a factory in the USA. The machining units, workpiece transfer and control systems were all new designs. In the initial concept, control programs were stored on magnetic tape cassettes, though the later version incorporated a full DNC system. While System 24 was not in the event commercially exploited, individual machines have continued to be used and there is little doubt that the concepts developed by Molins were the inspiration for other world-wide developments.

There were other early systems in Europe. In the German Democratic Republic, the machine industry consortium developed systems for rotational (gear wheel blanks) and prismatic parts: the ROTA and PRISMA systems. In the German Federal Republic, a system for printing machinery manufacture was installed at Heidelberg and this is now being expanded. It is believed that there are also systems in existence in Czechoslovakia and Bulgaria.

In the States, the major suppliers were Kearney & Trecker and Sundstrand, each having two systems running in the early 1970s. Cincinnati were also deeply involved but did not install any systems in industry: however, it is understood that they are now receiving orders.

In the 1960s Japanese companies had been quick to exploit DNC, systems being supplied by Fujitsu, Fanuc and Okuma. Complete systems were also developed, the main suppliers being Seiki, Toyoda and Toshiba, and some 18 systems with automatic workpiece transport are now in existence.

There are now over a hundred DNC systems in the States and at least the same number in Japan: DNC systems in these countries are part of the everyday manufacturing scene. In the UK investment in DNC and FMS has been minute. A couple of DNC systems have been installed based on NEL developments and several more systems are planned.

## Pressures motivating change

Recently a project called ASP (Automated Small-Batch Production) was commissioned by the Mechanical Engineering Machine Tools Requirements Board of the Department of Industry. A Committee of Industrialists (the ASP Committee) studied the developments abroad and recommended a programme of research and development for the UK.

An overall conclusion of the Committee was that the UK manufacturing industry, to survive, must raise productivity through cost-effective automation to at least the levels of other industrialized countries. They were also aware of increasing pressure in world markets from developing countries. Social factors, such as the wide disillusionment felt by those already in the engineering industry and reluctance of school-leavers to join, were also significant.

There are a number of pressures pushing the engineering industry towards higher use of computer aided manufacture. The ASP Committee detailed a number of these.

### 4.1 *Overseas competition*

Attempts are being made abroad to improve the world-wide low efficiency of small-batch production through higher investment and increasing levels of automation. While there is no absolute measure of efficiency in manufacturing industry much can be deduced by comparing the added value (output) produced per employee in this country with its competitors.

In the James Clayton Lecture to the Institution of Mechanical Engineers in 1976, Jones compared the average results of 416 Japanese manufacturing companies (covering nearly 2.4m employees) with 762 UK companies (covering some 4m employees) and concluded that the output per employee in the UK manufacturing industry was only 44 per cent of that in Japan. Nor is the situation improving. Figures show that the increase in capital invested in the same range of engineering manufacture in Japan per employee per year in 1974-75 was in the order of £4,500. In the UK it was £400. A comparison of the age of machine tools in the two countries highlights these figures starkly. In the UK 39 per cent of machines are under 10 years old. In Japan the figure is rising swiftly and is now 60 per cent. Japan is also increasing its total machine capacity by over 3 per cent per annum; the total number of machines in the UK has declined by 22 per cent in the last 10 years. The evidence of this investment can be seen in the small-batch production area and Japan is leading the world in applying and gathering experience in intermediate systems. Over 80 DNC systems are in use and at least 18 systems with automatic workpiece transport are working. Some 16,000 robots are in use today and annual production is gathering pace (3 000 today, 22 000 by 1980 and 66 000 by 1985). Many of them will operate in the small-batch area. In the USA over 100 DNC systems and 4 flexible manufacturing systems are in use and many more are planned. In the UK by comparison there are 3 DNC systems and no FMS systems. Having proved many of the concepts in their home markets both Japan and the USA are now exporting these systems, and systems are also being built or acquired in Sweden, East Germany, Bulgaria, Iran, India and Czechoslovakia.

These developments are being supported in the longer term by massive research and development programmes funded by governments. Japan has recognised the engineering manufacture industry as a major growth component of its economy because it seems ripe for development and automation.

### 4.2 *The export-low, import-high syndrome in the supply industry*

The National Economic Development Office in its recent report on the International price competitiveness, non-price factors and export performance states that:

'There is some sign that the UK, by comparison with France and particularly West Germany, tends to export relatively low valued products and import relatively high valued products within many industry categories and particularly within engineering sectors.'

The report shows the ratio of the average value per ton of German and French exports to the corresponding figure for British exports in some 35 industry sectors. The figure for the machine tool sector are the UK 100, Germany 199 and France 153. That is, German exports of machine tools have twice the value per ton of UK exports. The report also lists the ratio of the unit value of a country's imports to that of its exports in the same industry sectors. The figures for the machine tool sector are the UK 1.53, Germany 0.74 and France 1.04. (A ratio in excess of 1.0 means that the country imports products of a higher unit value than the products it exports.) Of the 12 mechanical engineering sectors listed, the UK imported goods with a higher unit value than its exports in 11.

In seeking explanations for these figures the report advances a number of hypotheses, one with particular relevance is:

'that the UK may be producing less technically elaborate products of older vintage that sell at a lower price for this reason although they are as good as other products in their class.'

The report then argues that:

'The production of less technically elaborate products does not necessarily prevent trade performance from improving. Less developed countries are almost certain to concentrate on production of both cheaper and more labour-intensive products.

What is important for their growth is the direction in which they are moving. Japan, for example, has moved from producing relatively simple products and making them in quite a labour-intensive way, to producing more complex products and using more capital-intensive methods of production. A number of developing countries now appear to be tracing the same sort of path. However, if a country moves progressively 'down market', then it is likely to find itself specialising increasingly upon products for which world demand grows more slowly as world income levels rise. There is only one way of avoiding this, and that is to become as efficient as possible in all aspects of the production and marketing of existing products and also to look out for opportunities to move 'up market'.'

In the context of the UK machine tool industry this argument seems valid and disquieting. Developing countries such as India, Taiwan and Israel are building up machine tool industries and now are looking for export markets. If the import/export figures for NC machines are taken as an indication of UK performance at the high technology end of the machine tool market, there is further evidence that all is not well. According to the 1977 Metalworking Production survey of machine tools, approximately 500 NC machines are imported into the UK per year, while some 200 are exported. There are also indications that the imports are of higher technology than the exports.

### 4.3 *Social and environmental factors*

There are a number of factors which are acting to limit or even reduce the number of skilled operators available for small-batch manufacture.

There are estimates that 60 per cent of the UK working population are now employed in the service industries and forecasts that if the UK follows the lead of the USA, over two-thirds of the workforce will be in service employment in 10 years time. There seems little doubt that we are moving inexorably towards what has been described as the post-industrial society.

There is some evidence that the average age of skilled machine operators is increasing and that significant numbers will leave manufacturing in the next few years through retiral. This tendency to move out of manufacturing is worsened by an apparent reluctance of school-leavers to serve craft apprenticeships.

The ASP Committee were not unduly pessimistic about this situation. They argued that if the UK is moving towards a service-type economy more men can be absorbed in that part, and it ought to concentrate on obtaining a stronger, (although perhaps somewhat smaller) manufacturing capacity based on much higher capital investment. Providing the flow from the manufacturing sector is approximately in balance with the growth in the service sector little unemployment should result.

### 4.4 *Health and safety factors*

Legislation is putting pressure on manufacturing industry to improve the working environment and in many cases to remove the operator entirely from the process of manufacture.

The use of higher cutting speeds made possible by new tool materials is a good example and it is likely that the full potential of ultra high speed cutting will not be achievable until the operator is removed from the vicinity of the cutting action. This of course is an incentive towards the adoption of automation with the corollary that those who do not automate will become less productive and less able to compete on world markets.

### 4.5 *Energy factors*

There is some evidence that reductions in total energy requirements can be made by the use of computer-controlled manufacturing systems. Savings will occur in machining rates, high machine utilization, smaller plant and timely modular replacement of worn or failed components of the system. Savings through redesign have not been included here although there is little doubt that the possession of a highly efficient manufacturing system will lead companies to consider their design procedures very carefully and in many cases will lead them to incorporate design into an integrated CAD/CAM system.

### Growth of computer aided manufacture

According to the Metalworking Production survey figures, the growth rate in NC machines in the UK has held steady at almost 10 per cent for the past few years. There are now 10 000 (out of a total of 900 000 machines) representing some 10 per cent by value of the total stock of machines.

At the worst, growth should continue at the 1 000 machines per annum giving a total of 23 000 machines by 1990. At the other extreme a geometric growth rate of 10 per cent (easily achieved by Japan in recent years) would give a total of 40 000 machines by 1990. The true total is likely to lie between these two limits, although closer to the bottom end, with some 2 000 machines being installed in the UK per annum by 1990.

A problem is to agree how many of these machines will be linked into systems, either DNC, workpiece transfer or both. The 1977 Delphi Forecast of Manufacturing Technology carried out by the Society of

Manufacturing Engineers predicted that 25 per cent of existing NC machines in the USA will be linked to central computers by 1987 and that by that time 15 per cent of the small and medium batch production in the USA will be from flexible manufacturing systems with workpiece handling.

These are impressive figures, although only forecasts, and any similar trend in the UK would result in large numbers of linked systems by the late 1980s. If we assume that the UK is some 10 years behind the USA in adoption of these techniques we arrive at a figure of some 800 NC machines per year linked into 100 systems by 1995.

### The ASP project

The Mechanical Engineering and Machine Tools Requirements Board, Department of Industry, approved an application by the National Engineering Laboratory in July 1976 for the funding of a project to study UK and International activity in small-batch automation and to recommend a programme of research and development.

The suggestion for this project had originally come from industry, stimulated by the developments abroad, and a Committee of Industrialists (the ASP Committee) was formed to direct a Working Party of specialist contributors. The Working Party members were set two main tasks by the Project Committee: first, as individual organisations, to study and report on particular topics relevant to the overall ASP concept; and second, as a group or in smaller teams, to consider the findings of the individual organizations and to further develop their ideas and concepts.

The study project was completed in December 1977, and the Report of the ASP Committee was endorsed in principle by the Requirements Board in March 1978. The ASP Committee found that the UK lags our major industrial competitors by about 10 years in the field of batch automation. They recommended as a short-term measure that industry should be encouraged to install several 'intermediate' systems – these would essentially comprise existing designs of NC machines linked by workpiece handling devices, all under computer control. Valuable experience would be gained in this way by both users and builders. At the same time, the UK meachine-tool industry should receive support for the first steps towards 'advanced' systems which should appear in the next five to ten years. An essential element of these advanced systems is considered to be highly reliable production units of modular design capable of operating unattended. A one-year study employing experienced designers from industry is being funded, and the outcome will be general arrangement drawings of this new generation of machine tools.

The ASP Committee also recommended that many existing research and development projects could make a significant contribution to the development of advanced systems if supported in a co-ordinated way; also new topics were suggested for funding. The Requirements Board has approved the continuation of the ASP Committee, with some modifications to its membership, and NEL will provide full-time project officers and co-ordinators.

Other aspects of manufacture were considered by the ASP Committee, and automated assembly of batches was considered to be particularly important. A decision on a study of automated batch assembly, similar to the ASP Project, has been deferred.

Further information on the ASP Project and copies of the ASP Technical Study and Bibliography may be obtained from the National Engineering Laboratory.

### Acknowledgements

This paper is presented by permission of the Director, National Engineering Laboratory, Department of Industry. It is Crown copyright reserved.

# Appendix    Glossary of computer terms

Algol
— a computer language used in programming many technical and scientific applications of the computer, Cf, Cobol, Basic, Fortran.

Analog computer
— a computer usually built for one particular application and which uses physical (usually electrical) properties analogous to the properties being studied (as a slide rule uses length as analogous to a number). These machines are most commonly used in process control Cf. digital computer.

Application program
— a program written by the computer user, or purchased by him, which carries out a complete function e.g. payroll processing, CAD etc.

Backing store
— an extension to the main store of a computer and physically distinct from it. The most common forms of backing store are magnetic disc, drum, and tape.

Basic
— a computer language, resembling natural English, which enables simple calculations to be programmed.

Batch processing
— a system of operation by which a computer may handle a succession of separate jobs with minimal or no operator intervention.

Bit
— unit of information (BInary DigiT) in a digital computer. 1 024 Bits is a Kilobit, sometimes abbreviated to "K" e.g. 64K.

Bureau — a computer bureau is a company that takes in clients' computer work either to help the clients' computer department during a period of peak load or to save the client from the cost of buying or renting his own machine and establishing the necessary support facilities.

CAD — Computer Aided Design.

Cobol — COmmon Business Orientated Language, a computer language used in programming the majority of commercial applications of the computer. Cf. Algol, Basic, Fortran.

Computer — an electronic device capable of processing information by executing a predetermined sequence of instructions.

Computer language — See *language*.

Compiler — a special program that translates the user-oriented computer language into the machine language. The compilers for high-level languages (Basic, Cobol, Fortran. Algol, etc.) are usually supplied by the computer manufacturers. See *system software*.

Console — the control (usually a teleprinter keyboard and associated switches) used by the operator to communicate with the CPU. The master terminal.

Core store — main storage medium which uses the magnetic properties of loops of ferrous material caught at the intersection of electric wires to store information. Being superceded by semiconductor storage.

CPU — Central Processing Unit or central processor, the main part of the computer, comprising of store, arithmetic unit, and control unit.

Data — one of the two classes of information that may be fed to a computer. Cf. program.

Data-bank — a file, or files, of data held on backing store and common to several different programs.

Digital computer — a computer in which information is handled in digitally coded form, i.e. as trains of electrical pulses. Its characteristics are the ability to process large numbers at very high speeds with a high degree of accuracy.

EDP — Electronic Data Processing – the use of digital computers or punch-card-handling equipment for manipulating information.

Fortran — FORmula TRANslation, a computer language used in programming many technical and scientific applications of the computer. Cf. Algol, Cobol, Basic.

Generation — *First generation computer*
An early machine built in the 1950s or early 1960s using valves.

*Second generation computer*
A machine built in the early or mid-1960s using transistors in place of valves.

*Third generation computer*
A machine built since the mid-1960s using micro-miniature circuits.

Hardware — the mechanical, electronic, magnetic and electrical parts of a computer system. Cf. software.

Input — the information that is fed into the computer, i.e. data or program. Sometimes loosely used for the punched tape or cards bearing the information, or for the action of feeding the information into the computer. Cf. output.

Language — a computer language is the form in which a programmer communicates with the computer. A low-level, or machine, language requires the programmer to have an intimate knowledge of the working of the computer. A high-level language (e.g. Algol, Cobol, Fortran) requires far less knowledge of how the computer works; consequently most programs are written in high-level languages. See *compiler*.

Light pen            – a pen-like implement that may be moved across the face of a visual display unit to enter new data or alter existing data.

Magnetic disc      – a form of backing store holding information on the flat surface of a disc or stack of coated discs on a common spindle. Information held on this type of backing store may be accessed almost as quickly as that in the main store.

Magnetic drum    – a form of backing store holding information on the coated surface of a drum which is physically as large as a disc-pack but holds only a tenth of the information. Access is faster than for disc.

Magnetic ledger card    – a conventional typed ledger card with a magnetic strip along one edge on which data is recorded and which can be read automatically.

Magnetic tape      – a form of backing store holding information on coated plastic recording tapes, that is less expensive than disc, but is slower, especially for random access of information which may require the whole tape to be re-wound.

Main store         – storage, or 'memory' connected directly to the CPU, and holding data and programs currently being used by the machine. Cf. backing store.

Main-frame computer    – a third generation computer which costs more than £100,000 and has a sophisticated range of programming languages and peripherals. It is estimated that less than 50% of the computer business will be of this form by 1980.

MICR             – a Magnetic Ink Character Reader will read typescript printed in magnetic ink.

Microcomputer    – CPU and storage chips mounted on a printed circuit board for incorporating as a control unit for a finished product e.g. NC machine tool. Cost approximately £50.

Microprocessor    – a CPU on a silicon chip.

Mini-computer — a third generation computer which costs £500-£100,000, and has less sophisticated hardware, software and maintenance qualities than mainframe machines e.g. programmed in BASIC only.

Modem — a device that allows a remote terminal to be used when connected to the computer over the normal telephone system.

MOS — Metal-Oxide-Semi-conductor the technology by which Large Scale Integrated circuits (LSI) are manufactured.

Multi-access — a system whereby several operators may, through remote terminals, each use the same computer facilities (files, programs, etc.) at the same time. Cf. time sharing.

Nanosecond — one-thousandth of a microsecond, i.e. $10^{-9}$ seconds.

NC machine tool — a device for cutting metal which is controlled by a program.

OCR — an Optical Character Reader will read printed, and in some cases hand-written characters.

Output — the information that emerges from a computer. Sometimes loosely used for the printed paper or other medium on which the information appears, or for the computer's action of passing the information to a peripheral device. Cf. input.

Peripheral — a terminal or backing store device attached to the CPU. This term includes all terminals, backing store units, modems etc.

Program — a sequence of instructions to be obeyed by the computer.

Programmer — a person who writes programs.

RAM — Random Access Memory, a storage medium which is accessed like a pigeon-hole system, rather than a roll of parchment.

Remote terminal — a terminal sited to be convenient to the user rather than convenient to the computer. It may be in the next office or on the next continent. Long distances are covered by use of telephone voice channels. See *modem, terminal.*

ROM — Read Only Memory, a storage medium in which information is held permanently, and which cannot be altered.

Semiconductor — a material, such as those based on silicon or germanium which can be arranged as an insulator or a conductor of electricity, dependent on the direction of an externally applied current.

Silicon chip — a fragment of a wafer of pure silicon, up to ⅛″ square, printed with alternate insulating, and semiconducting layers on which the pattern of an electronic circuit is etched e.g. main store or CPU.

Software — all computer programs, associated with the computer system, whether system or software, or application programs. Cf. hardware.

Systems analyst — one who analyses a function (e.g. of an office or department) and devises a system that will perform the same functions using computer techniques. This usually includes recommendation of a particular computer and peripherals and the production of basic software specifications.

System software — those programs, usually prepared by the hardware manufacturer, that provide the link between the application programs and the hardware. The term includes compilers for high-level languages (Algol, Cobol, Fortran, etc.) that allow user programs to be virtually machine-independent.

Terminal — a class of computer peripheral at which information may be transferred between the computer and an operator. These are:

| | |
|---|---|
| Card punch | Card reader |
| Paper tape punch | Paper tape reader |
| Teleprinter | Typewriter |
| Lineprinter | Graph printer |
| OCR | Visual display unit (VDU) |
| MICR | UDR |

Time sharing — a system whereby several operators may, through remote terminals, each use the same large computer at the same time so that each appears to have exclusive access to his own smaller computer. Cf. multi-access.

UDR — *Universal Document Reader*
A peripheral device that scans each sheet in a stack of standard printed forms and recognises special marks, made by a pencil, and feeds the information represented to the CPU.

UNIMATE — a programmable device which can be used to weld. Similar devices cut dies, body shells etc.

VLSI — *Very Large Scale Integration*
A future technology which requires manufacturing technologies involving electron beams, or X-Rays, to etch patterns on silicon chips.

Visual display unit (VDU) — a television-like terminal on which may be displayed script or line diagrams generated by the computer.